CW00349256

HITTING
AND
STOPPING

HOW I WON 100 FIGHTS

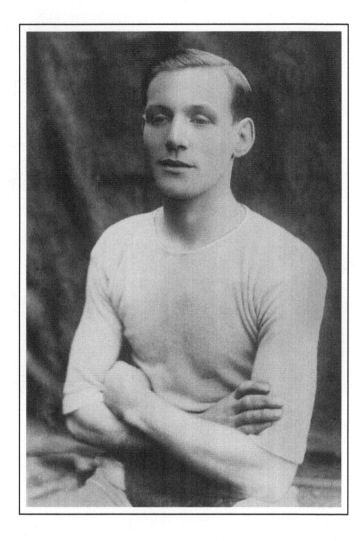

JIMMY WILDE
World Flyweight Champion
1916 - 1923

HITTING
AND
STOPPING

HOW I WON 100 FIGHTS

by

Jimmy Wilde

Peerless Press
Cardiff, Wales

First published 2012 by Peerless Press of Cardiff, Wales.
Cover design by A. Schupmann.
Internal page layout by Printondemand-Worldwide

Hitting and Stopping – How I Won 100 Fights

Copyright © Jimmy Wilde 2012

ISBN: 978-095703-421-1

A catalogue record for this book is available from the British
Library

An environmentally friendly book printed and bound in
England by www.printondemand-worldwide.com

This book is made entirely of chain-of-custody materials

Contents

List of Instructional Illustrations

11

14) A right back-hander to the jaw. This is the blow with which I coaxed Harry Brooks into exposing the jaw just before hooking with my left and winning with a knockout.

N.B. – The right was first crossed to miss intentionally and then back-handed. 83

Preface
(1914)

Jimmy Wilde's wonderful performances as a boxer have earned for him the title of "The Mighty Atom". He is only just over five feet in height, and turns the scale at 6st. 10lb. He is twenty-nine years of age, and in his short career has scored over one hundred victories, many of them gained at the expense of men more than two stone heavier than himself, and some 60 percent of them by the K.O. route.

By his defeat of Eugene Husson at the N.S.C. on March 13th in 1914, he secured the title of 7st. Champion of the World. In the words of one of our chief boxing experts, Jimmy Wilde is "the greatest boxer that ever happened."

Introduction

Jimmy Wilde was one of the greatest fighters the world has ever seen. Almost from the beginning of his boxing career, spectators tried in vain to describe the skill of a man made in miniature who defied conventional wisdom at every turn. In the history of the ring, it is hard to find a fighter so seemingly physically unprepared for the long journey to become one of the most revered boxing champions than Jimmy Wilde. When he first appeared on the fairground boxing booths of South Wales in 1908 he stood a shade over 5ft tall and bore a striking resemblance to a skeleton over which a thin layer of skin had been stretched. It was an easy enough task to count his ribs through his pale skin, and his arms were as spindly as broom handles. His delicate features made concerned onlookers guess that he was probably around ten years old.

The sixteen year old coal miner looked so weak and sickly that he caused great alarm to the booth patrons. Many feared that they would shortly be witnessing a massacre, which might leave the boy critically injured or even cost him his life. Some were quick to accuse the booth owner of brutality for even agreeing to let him fight. Those spectators that didn't object usually laughed. It was impossible to believe that the scrawny waif with the build of an undernourished greyhound stood a chance against any experienced challenger. None of the men gathered outside the boxing booth could have guessed that they were witnessing the start of the ring career of one of the most remarkable boxers since records began. Some would argue that Jimmy Wilde stands alone as the greatest pound for pound fighter of all time.

Despite having been advertised as weighing just 84 pounds (6st.) and barely out of his boyhood years, Wilde was soon knocking out experienced local fighters almost twice his weight with punches that travelled just a few inches. As a booth boxer, the cherubic fighter was expected to do battle against all comers, and for five years the 'Tylorstown Terror' as he became known, did just that, sending hundreds of opponents crashing to the canvas. His diminutive size ensured that he was never short of opposition. The majority were lucky to endure a couple of rounds before the unnatural strength of Wilde's punch stretched them out cold. The laughter from the booth patrons soon stopped. Amusement turned to wonder as the marvellous mite continued to floor comparative giants, often meeting several opponents each night. Locally, at least, the legend grew.

Jimmy Wilde, known as "The Tylorstown Terror",
"The Mighty Atom", and a few other ring names

Although his professional career is recorded as having commenced in 1910 at the age of eighteen, Wilde was already a battle tested veteran of the boxing booths by this time. The boxing booth had provided one of the hardest of training grounds then available, where the necessity to fight on such a frequent basis ensured that a fighter had to succeed or seek new employment. Wilde won, and kept winning.

This school of hard knocks toughened Jimmy to the degree that when he entered the professional ring, he remained unbeaten. In Wilde's first year as a professional he fought up to three times a month. Most challengers were left unconscious within a couple of rounds. When reports of the unstoppable fistic mite reached the ears of the sporting fraternity in London, few found the tale of the 'Terror' conceivable. It wasn't until 1912 that the Terror made his London debut. Even with victories piling up around his feet it was some task to convince promoters that the little Welshman had much chance of fighting his way through anything more substantial than a stiff breeze. It was for this reason that a nineteen year old Jimmy Wilde ended up making his first low-key appearance at a venue called 'The Ring' in Blackfriars rather than in the boxing theatre of the exclusive National Sporting Club at Covent Garden.

Luckily for Jimmy, The Ring's promoter, Dick Burge, had been swayed to give him an opportunity to showcase his skills by recent positive press reports. Thankfully Burge had not yet laid eyes on Wilde. Had he done so, as he later confessed, he would have shooed the pallid collier clean out of the building. The reminiscences of Bella Burge, Dick's wife, make for an accurate portrait of Jimmy's painfully undernourished appearance;

"...we laughed when we saw this scarecrowish-looking kid crawl through the ropes and shuffle about the ring to his corner. His frame was just a collection of bones with a skin drawn so tightly that at any moment one expected it to burst and a bone to pop out."

The audience appeared to be struck dumb with disbelief as Jimmy ambled to his corner and viewed the skeletal miner in utter silence. As had become commonplace, they were roaring with laughter a few moments later. Wilde was outweighed by 27lbs., and facing a formidable opponent in Matt Wells' 'Nipper', a capable fighter well known for bowling over a good collection of the local lightweights. There seemed to be no chance that Wilde would be able to stand up to his opponent, and a mischievous cry soon went up from ringside, warning; "Nipper, don't swallow the leek in one mouthful!"

Amusement gave way to wonder as Wilde proceeded to shower his man with punches from every conceivable angle at will. Nipper went down three times in the first round. After receiving the final right hand, his body stiffened as if shot. The Nipper did not get back up. The 93lb. fistic scarecrow was already making his way back to his changing room before anyone could believe the evidence of their own eyes.

Despite the discovery of such a pugilistic marvel, offers for future engagements were not quick in coming. In these days a tragedy in the ring was usually followed by the prosecution of the fighters and also included everyone involved in the organization of the match. The notoriously brusque manager of the National Sporting Club, Peggy Bettinson, was quick to reject any suggestion that Wilde might be approached to fight at the club, convinced that he would end up being charged with manslaughter. It wasn't until 1914 that Wilde's astonishing abilities became universally recognized following his knock out of the French champion Eugene Husson inside six rounds. London newspaper *The Times* was quick to herald the rise of a new boxing superstar, and concluded that Jimmy Wilde was the 'cleverest boxer living'. It was after this victory that Wilde's thoughts on boxing strategy and tactics, *Hitting and Stopping* was published, having originally been advertised under the title of *How I Won 100 Fights*.

Jimmy Wilde continued to pile up a dizzying number of victories and by 1916 had taken the British flyweight title. He took the World title in the same year, holding it until 1923. At the end of his career, Jimmy believed that the sum total of his fights including boxing booth battles numbered some 864 contests. Remarkably, he had been beaten on just a handful of occasions.

Did Jimmy Wilde have a secret? His abilities so far outstripped the bulk of his contemporaries that it is probably fairer to say that he had many. Wilde was a natural fighter, cast in a mould of his own. He was blessed with impossibly fast reflexes, and had a strange wiry strength unthinkable in one so small. His devastating punching power was complemented by a near perfect sense of timing and distance.

Throughout his career he was examined by doctors who were confounded in their attempts to discover the source of his incredible knockout power. Pictures of Jimmy reveal that while he was of seemingly fragile build, his broad shoulder and back muscles were developed beyond what might be deemed normal in a man of his size and weight. The foundation for this strength was almost certainly built in his early days in the coal mines. In this environment Jimmy had found that his slender frame was an advantage, enabling him to slide into narrow gullies where larger men could not fit. Working at the coalface with his heavy pick at unorthodox angles assisted him in developing unnatural strength in his stick like arms.

In the ring his methods were completely his own. Despite his compact size, his strategy was built on the principle that attack is the best form of defence. In the boxing booths, where he might have to fight multiple opponents each night, the necessity to conserve energy and dispatch challengers as quickly as possible had been vital. The confined quarters of the 12ft fairground boxing ring probably played a significant part in honing his wraithlike sense of distance.

One minute he was banging in crisp, hard punches that were snapping back the heads of men stones heavier. In the next moment he had evaporated, reappearing out of reach of his opponent's desperate counters. His hands hung down below his waist, but his apparent vulnerability was deceptive. Jimmy's strength was such that even from a relaxed position he could strike with punches that could knock a man clean off his legs, yet often came in flurries so fast that they couldn't be counted.

Wilde developed uncanny speed when fighting at close quarters. He favoured keeping close to his opponent, preferring to avoid blows with a sway of the body or a slight birdlike twitch or turn of the head rather than by relying solely on footwork to propel him out of harm's way. By dodging rather than blocking punches, and making his opponent miss, he tired his opponent down while conserving his own energy, a vital consideration for a man of his size. A minimal shift in his position meant that he was able to counter without having to move back into range. This was only possible because Jimmy's judgment of distance bordered on the sublime. By minimizing unnecessary movement, Jimmy was able to make his man miss by fractions while leaving him in a position that ensured he was able to punch with all his strength.

His footwork followed the same principles and he never expended more energy than was necessary, his curious shuffling style gliding him in and out at a moment's notice. By keeping his feet in close proximity to the ground Wilde ensured he was always balanced and able to punch whenever he saw an opening. The accuracy of his blows was such that he rarely let a punch go that didn't find its target. On many occasions throughout his career, Jimmy made fast fighters appear slow. His superior speed was central to his formula for success, enabling him to materialize almost at will within an opponent's reach and attack with pinpoint precision before effortlessly returning to a position of safety.

His spectral ability in defence allied to his terrific punch earned Jimmy Wilde his most famous ring name, that of 'The Ghost with the Hammer in his Hand'. Over the years, many ring names tried to describe some measure of his genius, 'The Mighty Atom', 'The Indian Famine', 'The Tetrarch of the Ring', 'The Human Hairpin', 'The Welsh Wizard' and the 'Streak Of Lightning'. None seemed to fully encapsulate the wonder that Jimmy Wilde provoked in those spectators lucky enough to have seen him in his prime. In the history of boxing it is hard to find a fighter who gave away such vast chunks of weight, while fighting so frequently and stopping his opponents so conclusively.

It seems unlikely that a reading of *Hitting and Stopping* will provide a blueprint to replicate Jimmy Wilde's genius in the ring, without the attributes that made him unique. For referee Eugene Corri, who presided over many of Wilde's famous contests, Jimmy's style was beyond analysis, and Corri concluded that, '...it is hopeless to attempt to describe the achievements of a man who is not like other men'. The same might be said of Jimmy's methods, they suited him and his uncanny abilities. It is doubtful that any amount of training could create a fighter made exactly in his image.

Readers of *Hitting and Stopping* can learn a great deal regarding the strategy and ring craft of one of the greatest fighters ever known. Whether or not a close understanding and absorption of Jimmy Wilde's thoughts can ever result in such unparalleled success in the ring as he enjoyed remains to be seen. For the writer of this introduction, it seems unlikely. In his lifetime, Wilde was described as a freak, a marvel and a mystery. The root of his genius continues to defy explanation. There will always be great fighters, some go on to become great champions, but there will never be a giant killer that could rival the deeds of a tiny Welsh coal miner by the name of Jimmy Wilde.

So why, nearly a hundred years after the original publication of Wilde's *Hitting and Stopping* is there a need for a new updated edition? Having recently attempted to record some part of the lives of some of the forgotten ring men to have come from South Wales in the book *Mountain Fighters, Lost Tales of Welsh Boxing*, it seemed a shame to leave the insights of one of the greatest fighters of all time to be relegated to the past.

Like most great boxing tales, Jimmy Wilde's story transcends the ring itself. The tale of the 'Mighty Atom' deserves to be remembered, and should continue to inspire us even a century after the beginning of his astonishing boxing career. Beyond the boxing strategies contained within, there is much that we can learn from Jimmy. That one of the smallest men to enter the ring could become one of the greatest should stand as one of the most important lessons that can be learned. Courage, self-belief and determination can bring remarkable results. We should never fear to fail, we should square our shoulders and put all of our efforts towards reaching our goals, in doing so we determine our own destiny. They laughed when Jimmy slid between the ropes more skin and bone than bulk and muscle. It didn't matter. Jimmy fought on, until he had conquered the world and won the hearts of those that had once doubted him.

Resolute determination and the will to succeed makes the impossible possible. No matter whether we fight our battles within the ring, or outside it, we should, as Jimmy himself said, 'fight as hard as you can'... and never, ever, give in. It is, perhaps, Jimmy Wilde's greatest lesson

Lawrence Davies

Hitting And Stopping

Chapter One
Get In and Get Away

The old rule of the prize ring which has been handed down to the glove-fighters of to-day enjoins its professors to hit, stop and get away. It was a most excellent rule, I suppose, and still is a fairly sound one, but from my own experience I should say that the second part of it is really unnecessary.

The hitting part of it is all right, and so is the getting away from a return blow (if one is smart enough to do so), but why boxers should be asked in the same breath to do the latter and also to guard the return is one of those mysteries which it is impossible to fathom.

Why on earth should any man waste his strength and energy and run risks in an attempt to block a blow which he can dodge? Firstly, because he may fail to block the blow and may actually *stop* it either with his face or body instead of with his arm or glove, and that kind of stop is neither profitable nor pleasant.

On the other hand, the advocates of the stop business may argue that a man who is always getting away is almost certainly wasting, or rather, neglecting opportunities, since there is no riper moment for a punch than that which occurs just after one's adversary has failed to land. These will further insist that the man who is always getting away is consequently always getting out of range, and that since he must come back within hitting distance if he wants to score, he will necessarily lay himself open to being scored off. But they forget that it is not really necessary to dance back away in order to avoid a blow. The man who cares to practise the art of ducking and swerving can escape being hit, and yet stay well within range. Now and then it may not be bad policy to dodge clean away, and thereby to make one's opponent miss by a foot or a yard, because a really bad miss is apt to not only discourage him, but also to make him lose his balance; but, as a rule, it is far wiser to keep close and to rely on ducking, and on sudden twists and turns of the head and body.

I always make a practise of keeping close in, and yet, if I may say so without boasting, have rarely been hit, that is, hit hard. Of course, now and then one cannot avoid getting in the way of a punch which one would much rather have escaped altogether. Bouzonnie, for instance, hit

*Drawing back from a lead by a simple
sway back of the body from the hips.*

me pretty sharply some time back, at Liverpool, but then I was giving a good deal of weight away and had not fully grasped his style.

I may also add that I did not particularly object to being hit by him. He had started off in a great hurry and at top speed, plainly in an almost feverish hurry to put me out before I could get going, and so it was up to me to weaken him a trifle before I started out to bustle him. As he was both a bigger and a stronger man, and by no means a dob either, it was necessary to be rather careful with him. I had to get home on him and to hurt him, and above all I wanted to get the fight finished before it had gone its full distance.

He had, I expect, heard all about me, and knew that I had a reputation for stopping my opponents and even for knocking out men who were anything from one to two stone heavier than myself, so that unless I could lure him into leaving openings it might be that I should never be given a chance to score a knock-out punch; and I always like, for various reasons, to knock my opponents out. You see, I have been rather in request lately, and I daresay that I could if my hands would only allow me, fight two or three times every week, though, if I were to be content with winning all my contests, on points, the offers might diminish in number, besides which it is quite certain that my strength and stamina would follow a similar route.

Side-stepping a left lead and crossing the right to the chin.

It may be all very well to wear the name of "Terror" and to be looked up to with awe, even if the people who do so are able to look down on you physically, but there are penalties attaching to the "Terror" business, and by no means the least of these is the necessity of having to live up to one's title. One cannot very well go around collecting good fees for being terrible if one only leaves one's verdicts to the referee every time.

So when I met Bouzonnie I had various inducements either to put him out or make him quit, and the only way I could see of punishing him severely enough to do either was by breaking down any cautious reserve he might feel. If he had any idea that I was going to put one across on him he would be sure to dodge around, keep his distance, rely on his reach and keep up as strong a defence as he could. So I did my best to convey the idea that I had been somewhat overrated, and he accepted the suggestion. In fact, he bustled me pretty severely for the first two or three rounds and until he had lost most of the respect which he had been advised to feel for me. He charged me over and thumped me hard, and was just beginning to fancy that he was going to be the first to chalk up a defeat on my record, when I went all out for him.

He saw that it was going to be a real fight from then on, and he was getting rather fond of the idea that he would have the best of matters

*Pushing down the left hand with the right
and shooting the left to the face.*

if we started to mix things. I am quite certain that for a round or so he really believed that I was desperate, and that he had forced me to fight for all I was worth in the belief that this was the only way I could escape being put out, and it was just then that he found out that he was up against things.

If I had started out at top speed earlier, it is by no means impossible that he would have got away and given me all sorts of trouble. But as he was travelling fast, and had got into full swing, he wasn't able to change his methods, and - well, I daresay you know what happened.

I got close and kept close. I was hitting faster and harder than he was, and was also dodging most of his returns, and, though he explained afterwards that he had no desire to "quit" when Mr. Jack Smith thought that he had given in, yet, without vanity, I believe that the contest would not have lasted much longer in any case.

It will have been noticed that though I am always sent against boys and men who are much bigger and heavier than myself, and also that I have, in all my career, only once met a smaller opponent (when I met Eugene Husson at the National Sporting Club, to be precise), yet I invariably make a practice of keeping as close to my opponents as I possibly can. Of course, I get charged over sometimes. I cannot help that. But I do not often get knocked off my feet.

For one thing, I suppose that I was born with a natural aptitude for the game, and, for

*Coaxing an opponent to lead with the left
so as to secure an opening for a right cross.*

another, I can honestly say that I have been lucky enough to have the best coaching and practise that could be desired. Somehow or another I was always fairly fast, and I may say right off that the most important department of the boxing game is speed. Our heavies, middles, welters and men at lesser weights would win more laurels than they do from French and American rivals if they would only recognise the fact that, after all, pace is nearly everything.

Not quite everything, of course, because mere pace is apt to prove of small value unless it can be maintained and is supplemented with real punching power. Quick, rapid hitting and smart defence will enable a man to gain points and may win him success over the average run of competitors, but sooner or later every boxer will run up against an opponent who will not mind being outpointed so long as he can punish in return. Given strength, stamina, and a real wallop, this type of man will in time nearly always be able to wear the other fellow down, especially if that other is merely a gentle tapper, whose blows are incapable of shaking or hurting the man on whom they land.

One of the very worst mistakes which the average boxer makes is to believe that pace detracts from force. It is true that Fred Welsh does not carry a particularly hard punch around in his luggage, and it is equally true that he is one of the fastest men ever seen in the ring; but his lack of punching power is in no

*Ducking under a left hook and securing
an opening to hook the right to the face.*

way due to the speed at which he travels, though I have often heard it declared and seen it written that the rarity of Welsh's knock-out triumphs can be easily explained by the fact that, owing to the tremendous speed at which he travels, he is unable to "set" himself properly for a really forcible delivery.

I believe, too, that a very similar criticism has been levelled at Packey McFarland, and that it has been pointed out that Packey has of late scarcely ever knocked a man out. Yet McFarland can hit quite hard enough whenever he wishes to do so, as I am quite sure Jack Goldswain would be one of the first to testify, and I am inclined to doubt whether Packey ever boxed faster and at the same time hit harder than he did when he met Goldswain.

Take Jim Driscoll as an example. Jim was surely every bit as fast as either Welsh or McFarland, and yet he could always score a knock-out whenever he wanted one. Driscoll never needed to "set" himself in order to deliver a really telling punch. That is to say, he was not obliged to twist or shift himself into any particularly position for the purpose. He was always "set", and could put in all the hard punch he wanted the moment he saw the right opening.

There is a reason for this, of course, or perhaps a double reason. In the first place, Driscoll would be always ready, always expecting to see an opening present itself, and was always ready to grasp it when it came; and, secondly, he would have been working for openings all the time-mainly for the one which he finally seized; but, anyhow, for *an* opening-and, being conscious that he might not always secure the one he had been calculating on, careful to keep himself fully prepared to take full advantage of anything which might turn up.

Punching power is an indefinable thing. That is to say, it is by no means easy to explain either where it comes from or why it goes. A man may look like a terrific puncher. He may have a magnificent pair of shoulders, with all the hitting muscles well in evidence, and yet may not be able to punch a hole in a pat of butter. Another man may have arms like pipe stems, no particular shoulders or muscular development worthy of mention, and yet he may be endowed with the kick of a mule.

Again, one frequently comes across men who have either found a punch or else lost one. A mere ordinary tapper who has never been known to possess a punch worth mentioning will suddenly develop a wallop before which opponent after opponent will go down, while another whose victories were gained solely through his tremendous hitting powers will become unable to hurt anyone. Neither of these can tell how the change came. The first has simply found a punch and the other has lost one. That is all.

Punching power can be cultivated, however, and, it may be added, that it is not always the man whose blows look so terrific who really hits the hardest. The secret of hard hitting is, after all, merely a case of accurate timing: the ability to land straight and crisply with the full spring of the muscles, at the exact moment when the recipient is swinging in (unintentionally, of course) to meet the blow. That is the sort of thing which puts a man down on the boards.

The knock-down blow, even a knock-out punch, need not travel very far. A few inches will be all sufficient, although it is true that many of my own digs, my hardest blows, cover a considerably greater distance. But then that is because I am forced to hit upwards on many occasions - at faces which are several inches further up in the air than my own.

Otherwise, I rarely have to shoot out an arm to its fullest extent. I am, as a rule, so close to my man that I can snap one home any time I want to do so. This saves time, and also enables me not only to economise time, but also the effort of driving my punches through the air.

I believe that I make more use of my feet than Pedlar Palmer used to find necessary, but then there is a double reason for this. I may or may not be half as clever at ducking and dodging, at bobbing and bending as he was in this respect. But then it should be remembered that Palmer rarely gave, and was rarely asked to give, much weight away to his opponents, whereas I am usually matched with boys who are as I have pointed out already, anything from half a stone to a stone and a half heavier. And so I have to cultivate speedy footwork to a marked extent, if only to withdraw myself from the sudden charges of much bulkier frames, which might, perhaps, sweep me off my feet, with possibly disastrous results if I had not dodged out of the way in time.

My dancing, my in-and-out footwork, moreover, has another use. For by springing backwards and forwards I find that I get a most useful send-off for my punches, and am able to make them so much more effective. I scarcely fancy that I need to point out that my ability to punch hard had taken me further than any other ability I may possess. I do not know whether I am so superlatively skilful, I suppose I am cleverer than the ordinary run of boxers. But I really believe that my success has been chiefly due to the fact that I can punch harder than many lightweights, despite my damaged hands.

My chief aim is to keep as close to an opponent as I can. I rarely if ever clinch, and I do not think anybody can accuse me of ever holding a rival. Nor do I allow my rivals to hold me. I may occasionally get back out of hitting distance, but if I do, it is only for the fraction of a second. I am always back inside it again with the very next sway of my body or motion of my feet. If I do play a continually getting in and getting out game, I think I may safely assert that I am more often "in" (i.e., inside hitting distance) than out of it.

I am in the game to win my contests as quickly as I can and to win as many of them as I can. In one respect I am unfortunate in that I am so small. I can earn good money, but I cannot get hundreds of pounds every time I go into a ring, while I am afraid that I can never look forward to a day when I shall be offered thousands for contests of any length or description.

So you see I have to keep busy if I am to put anything really substantial away for my old age. People tell me that I ought to rest up, and that I am foolishly reckless to fight as frequently as I do. It is true that I am not able to give my hands the rest I guess they deserve and need; but, then, on the other hand, I really cannot afford to lay off. As I am not able to make big sums, I have got to make as many small or moderate ones as I can, if only out of regard for my stamina.

And for the same reason I do as little stopping as I can. It is far less exertion to me to just remove myself out of the way of a punch, provided of course that I only slip it by a duck or swerve of the head. It is also more annoying to my opponents, and I may add that it exhausts a man more to miss altogether than it does to have his punches warded off.

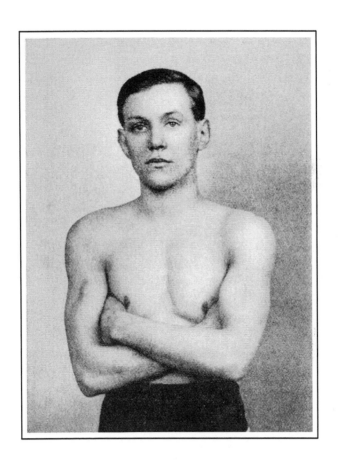

Chapter Two
On Hitting

The average spectator of a boxing contest would appear to be much more forcibly impressed by seeing a terrific swing which swishes through the air and lands with a resounding smack than he is when he sees a short snappy punch which has travelled, say, from six to twelve inches, and which makes very little noise when it arrives.

So it seems worthwhile stating that the loud blows are rarely the ones which do any particular damage. It is the crisp one which sends that shiver down a man's spine: the shiver which goes right down to his heels, and which leaves him open and gasping, and unable to dodge or avoid a series of stinging jabs and snappy jolts which ought to-but which do not always follow.

All punches ought to be as hard as they can be made-time, position and other circumstances being duly taken into account. Every boxer, I suppose, is fully aware of this, though I am sorry to say that only a very few boxers here and there would seem to remember it when engaged in a serious contest. For time and again you will see a man sending in blows, with plenty of time and through openings which are as wide as anyone could desire, into which he has not put one-half the force of which he was capable. He may and possibly has put all the display and more than two-thirds of all the energy of which he was capable into them, but the force, the snap, the real telling power has been conspicuous chiefly by its absence.

It may have been a wild slam which he has just let go at a target which he hopes will prove to be well within range when his blow lands, or he may have hit without thought at all and with only a very moderate amount of hope. In other words, he has "set" himself for the punch, perhaps, and in his eagerness to duly "set" himself has left everything else to sheer chance. Too many boxers, in fact, I might say the vast majority of British boxers, devote so much attention to the expenditure of all their muscular strength and energy into the delivery of a blow that they forget to pay sufficient attention either to its direction or to its timing.

The punches which tell, the real winning punches, are much simpler affairs than the terrific swings which draw long "O-o-h's" from the groundlings. The short snappy affairs, shot in from short range with the full swing of all the body and all the drive of the leg muscles behind them, are the genuine winners.

*Another duck under a left hook and securing
an opening for a punch to the ribs or body.*

They should never miss, unless they are intended to miss (and I propose to devote a full chapter to the subject of intentional misses), firstly, because a missed punch means a foolish waste of most valuable energy, and secondly, because a miss, especially a bad miss, means that one has laid oneself open to more or less serious reprisal.

In judging a boxing contest points are given for defence as well as for attack. Every boxer knows that, or ought to know it; but the trouble is that so many boxers waste time, energy and thought in playing "gallery" defence. That is to say, that they will dance about out of range and duck or swerve from a dozen to a score of times in succession, with the sole intention of drawing a round of applause, and perhaps several peals of laughter from the gallery, under the impression that their cleverness and dodginess will be remembered and in the minds of those who recall it may outweigh most of the real solid work on the other side.

The argument is a pretty one and a fairly attractive one to the arguer, but is based on a mistaken idea, because boxing memories are about the shortest in the world, *and* also the one man's whose memory really counts, viz., the referee's, is usually a somewhat unemotional one. The average referee has seen so much gallery play in his time that he has come to rate it at its true value and to resent it in consequence. He knows, he cannot help

Stepping in swiftly under a left hook or swing, pushing an opponent's left up, blocking the right with the elbow and at the same time upper cutting with the left to the chin.

knowing, that it has been introduced with a view to impress the onlooker with an inflated sense of its value; and since he knows himself to be the only onlooker who really counts, he is rather inclined to regard it as an insult to his own intelligence.

Yes, the sport of boxing may be the Noble Art of Self Defence, but as far as the scoring part of it is concerned it is Attack or Offence which is the winner every time. And besides, a strong attack is always the best and surest defence, for the simple reason that if the other man's time and attention are fully occupied in protecting himself he will have very little chance of carrying out offensive operations on his own account.

Yet if a man is going to make a strong attack and is going to rely on his powers of attack both to win and also to keep the other fellow from scoring points-which will suggest that he has at least a right to consideration when the verdict is being arrived at-then must that man look to it that his attack is not only rapid, but also heavy and sustained. The offensive-defensive line must be kept going. There must or should be no easing up, and if an attack is going to be all these things, or is even going to approach the ideal, then it must of necessity be pushed home-in other words, carried on from the shortest of ranges.

There are past masters of the defensive-offensive method, like Fred Welsh, who can play

Having lured an opponent's guard down
you can step in quickly and upper cut to the chin.

the blocking game to perfection, and who consequently prefer to convert a boxing contest into a more of less aggravated clinch; but I have a shrewd suspicion that once these close in-fighters run up against a man of their weight and class who can play the fast open game, then they and all the other great in-fighters are really booked for defeat.

They may block, hold and release, back-hand, slip in sly jolts and digs and pull off all the wiles and stratagems which they have studied and perfected, but they are going to be in for a warm time unless their opponents elect to play them at their own game.

For they must coax their opponents into joining in with them at the semi-holding and hitting game. Half, perhaps even three-fourths, of their success is due to the fact that they are skilful enough to force their adversaries to hamper themselves in the vain effort to counter the in-fighter's tactics. One cannot, for instance, accuse the in-fighter of holding, so much as of a series of holds and releases. He will trap his rival's arm, commence the semblance of a wrestle and then let go, plant a punch, check the other fellow again, *then* let the other man hold, or rather force him into fastening a clutch himself. So very much of it is not only half-arm work, but elbow hitting.

I don't mean by that that the in-fighter digs with the point of his elbow, though very few indeed of them are at all particular as to

A swift step in and hooked lead to the face.

whether they punch with their elbows, wrists, forearms, shoulders or even head; but that the majority or at least half their blows are "flipped" from the elbow, and consequently lack the force which comes with a straight drive or hook which carries the weight of the shoulder and possibly the body as well behind it.

It is true that the tip-top in-fighters hit tremendously fast as a rule. (Remember that I am referring now to the real champions at the close quarter business, the Fred Welshes and the leading Americans, and that I am quite aware that the vast majority of so-called in-fighters are slower than any funeral) But these express speed gentlemen rarely hurt for all their pace. They flip, backhand and slap; it would be gross flattery to describe any blows of this kind as actual punches.

It is true that the back-hander is at times a fairly useful blow, but only because it can be converted into a very annoying and at times a disconcerting visitation. As a painful infliction it is hardly worthy of mention.

The only brand of punch which will ever win a real contest from a formidable opponent must be sent home with the knuckle part of the gloves, and really there is no reason at all why any boxer should attempt to connect with any other portion of his hands. The knuckle punch not only hurts the receiver more, but possesses the extra advantage of saving the hands of the

A side-step and push round of an opponent who is covering up and who cannot be otherwise punched.

If this move is carried out correctly and the elbow pressed sufficiently the body will be laid open to a left swing or hook.

puncher, since the force of the impact is distributed over the full length of the arm.

The advocates of the swinging delivery may counter this statement with the reminder that I have confessed to damaged hands myself, and I must admit that both my "mauleys" are considerably the worse for wear. But then-well, just think of the work I have given them to do during the last few years. I am open to bet that mine are the only pair of hands now in active use which could have withstood the strains imposed on them during that period without going right out of commission. As it is they need a rest very badly, and, as I cannot afford to give them one, I have to nurse them in a manner of my own which I will describe later.

I have referred previously to the advantages of quick hitting, and may add that I do not believe that I should have earned half the reputation which has been accorded me if I had not developed the ability to jab home four or five lefts or rights in succession to the same spot. One has to keep pegging away, feinting and sparring until one secures an opening, and openings do not always come like leaves in autumn; but, when they do arrive, it is foolish to be content with just one punch through them.

Snap home the first, whether left or right, and let this be sufficiently sharp to give the recipient pause. As a rule, the first punch will come rather as a surprise (for if he had been

Forcing a capture of the interior lines.

expecting the blow there would have been no opening). And then before he can recover, ram home a couple more. If your first punch has been delivered correctly, either as a straight drive from the shoulder with the drive of the left and body muscles behind it, or failing that, if it has been whipped in from short range, with an action rather similar to that of cracking a whip, the other man's hands will almost inevitably go up. The chin may even be exposed, and you may be able to either cross him or hook him on it.

But if by any chance he should have covered up his danger zone, it is more than probable that you will have the whole area of his body exposed to your attack, and it will only need a sharp prod to the wind or stomach to bring the guard down and to furnish you with another opening to get home on the jaw.

It may be said that it is an easy task to lay down a simple plan of campaign like this, but far from easy to carry out the plan. Perhaps it is, but the carrying out is much less difficult that you might think. There are two or three essential points to bear in mind. The first is that it is always advisable to get in as close to one's opponent as one can. One should be able to get close in while one is feinting, or else to dart in following the delivery of a straight left lead; and, once in, one should make a careful point of keeping close in, unless very important reasons, such as a serious jab or a heavy

Covering up and stepping in to secure the interior lines.

*Note that both face and body are fully protected
and that I am opening up my opponent's body for attack.*

punch, for instance, recommend a more liberal use of the ring.

But if one has to go away, either in order to recover from punishment, as a feint, or for any tactical reasons, it is always best to get back close again and to keep close, for the very simple reason that unless one is close up any amount of time and numerous opportunities will be wasted.

Point number two is that the knack of hard, clean, snappy hitting should be cultivated to the fullest possible extent. Every blow delivered should hurt, and hurt badly. They ought, if possible, to jar and even to shake the recipient up pretty badly. It is perhaps too much to ask that every punch should be a winning one, but that should be the ideal aimed at.

Point number three, without the cultivation of which, I am afraid, the first essential will prove a rather disastrous piece of my strategy, is that the quick manipulation of the head and body must be brought as near perfection as possible. For it stands to reasons that if one is always within close hitting distance one is also always liable to be hit and hit hard.

Be careful to avoid overdoing the ducking and dodging business. Do not waste time and do not waste effort. Bring more intelligence to bear on your shadow boxing practise. For I am inclined to think that the average boxer goes through his shadow sparring in most perfunctory fashion, and in fact shadow boxes rather as a physical exercise than as a cultivation of boxing ability. To these I would say: Try the following method in future: Do not just fix your mind on the things you are doing or want to do to your imaginary opponent, but mix these up with a few notions as to the things he will be trying to do to you. Fancy that he is close up to you and that you are in trouble, and then see if you cannot get out of that trouble without having to clinch or hold him. Play both *roles* yourself and you will find that you can work both ways. That is to say, you will discover the mistakes you are liable to make yourself in actual combat. You will find that you have ducked the wrong way and have laid yourself open to an upper cut or fierce jab, and you will also note that you have missed several really good openings for punches yourself.

I feel that I have not expressed myself as clearly as I could have wished to do here. But then these things are not easy to explain on paper. Yet I honestly believe that if you try this method seriously and conscientiously you will be able to make something of it, and also to get a fuller grasp of my meaning. In any case, if you have done nothing else, you will at least have trained your mind to think, and that is the chief fault with the boxers I have seen in action. They either do not think at all or else they do not think nearly enough, having quite forgotten that the game of boxing is, more a conflict of wits than of anything else.

Then again, in your sparring practise with your partners in the gymnasium, make a point of working in close. You can arrange it with them that they shall cut out the holding and clinching business. And if they will not, well, just give them the sack and find some others. Though it must be confessed that a clinching sparring partner now and then has his uses as well, since he will assist you to cultivate the knack of either slipping out of a clinch, or of persuading the other fellow to cut out the clinching business altogether if he doesn't want to get hurt.

Don't come back at me, for goodness' sake, with the statement that it takes two to make a fight, and that if the other fellow will persist in holding, clinching, and wrestling you will be more or less compelled to do the same, because you can always prevent any opponent from clinching too excessively, save, of course, on those occasions when he simply flings his arms round you and holds on like grim death, tooth and nail, and then-well, the referee will soon intervene and finish the fight for you by turning the other chap out of the ring. How many times have you seen Jim Driscoll allow another man to hold and clinch himself? Have you seen either thing happen half a dozen times in all his career?

For don't forget that the other man must throw his arms around you if he is going to hold. And then what are your own arms doing to allow it? You can or should be able always to block or stop those arms from establishing any sort of clutch by interposing your own forearms against his. And then, if you are at all quick, you can send in a number of jabs, jolts and digs to his body, with an occasionally snappy punch or so to his face, just as reminders, before you slip away and return to unhampered movement.

But you are not going to do any of these things successfully; you are not going to prevent the other fellow from running any fight on the lines which suit him best unless all your punches sting and hurt. Bear that in mind. And make it the first rule, the very first rule of everything, that every time you hit you will hit with the fullest power of possess. The angle may be an awkward one, your position at the moment may be an awkward one, your position at the moment may not be one which you would have chosen if you had had your full choice in the matter. It doesn't matter. None of these things really matter so long as all your practise, whether it be at shadow boxing, sparring, ball punching or actual ring combat has been directed to the extraction of every ounce of hitting energy you possess.

Gather up your punching power from your heels. Let it pass up through your legs, loins, back muscles and whip it down with your arms into your fists as they connect with the other man's face or body. Punching power, you know, is mental rather than physical, and if you have made up your mind that every punch you send in is going to hurt and to hurt very badly, then every one of your punches will do so. It is almost entirely a matter of will power, and is, after all, the easiest and simplest branch of boxing to cultivate.

Finally, and it is finally because I believe it to be the last and also the most important thing which I can say on the subject of hitting, do devote extra special attention to developing the punching force of your straight left leads. Over and over again one sees really good left-handers, men who can plant their left leads almost as quickly and as accurately as anyone could wish to see them planted. One sits up and takes notice and says to oneself: "Here at last is a man who should be able to more than hold his own with any Frenchman or American." And then one sees the other fellow take the left leads as though they were snowflakes, walk right past and through them to welt the body good and hard, and send the left-hand tapper down to the boards.

And right there one has an object lesson in the decay of English boxing. Some of our fellows are as pretty and as accurate in their left-hand work as any of the old-timers were; but they haven't even the beginning of a punch. They *push* their hands out, and quite a number of them get back as they do so.

They are wasting time, wasting their own strength and energy and recklessly wasting their opportunities. The man who can't hurt, who can't check an opponent every time he shoots his left out to the face, ought to start to learn boxing all over again, or else quit the game altogether, for he hasn't learnt the first rudiment of the game.

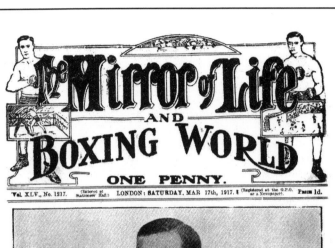

Chapter Three
On Stopping

I have suggested that, after all, stopping a blow is an almost negligible branch of the business, but on looking over all that I have written on the subject I am rather inclined to fancy that I have somewhat overdone things.

It is, of course, always better and more profitable from every point of view to avoid, to duck, dodge or slip a punch than to waste time and to risk bruises to one's arms in parrying them; but, all the same, there are some punches which must be warded off, since there is no other method, at the moment, whereby they can be prevented from reaching one's face or body, where they will exert a much more unpleasant effect. So let us put the thing this way: Avoid all the punches you can, and only try to parry those which you cannot avoid.

Next, make a point of trying to block blows rather than parry them. You won't strain yourself so much, and you will both annoy and weary the other fellow more by so doing.

For one thing, he may have "set" himself for the punch by the slow, laborious process beloved by the average boxer which wastes so many opportunities and which entails so hard a strain on the nerves and muscles. If he has done this, then it does not need much argument to point out that the shock of finding his blow checked just as it is starting will react badly both on his nerves and on his brain. You will have brought him up sharply at a round turn and that is going to jar him, and to jar him pretty badly.

Of course, one has to be fairly quick if one wants to get these blocks and checks in in time. One has to forsee that a punch is coming, and one has to forsee the kind of punch it is going to be. But then the man who cannot forsee this sort of thing, and forsee it both accurately and quickly, is never going to make any very great name for himself at the boxing game. That is why there are so many boxers down among the ruck and so few up at the top of the tree. I suppose that some of us are incapable of seeing ahead, but I am afraid that those who cannot have been too lazy to cultivate their powers of perception. We do these things more by instinct than by anything else, you know. There is something rapping inside my head when I am fighting which seems to tell me in advance just exactly what the other fellow is going to do-and I don't know that I am such an extraordinary freak of Nature as to be the only boxer so gifted.

You have only to watch any of the top notchers at the game and you will see that they have got their parries, their ducks and their counters well under way almost before their opponents have started operations. You can't say that they have reasoned things out, for the simple reason that they haven't had the time. In a good many cases they have started their counter, their block, their duck or their swerve without being actually conscious of what they were doing. It is purely a matter of instinct with us. At least, that is the impression I have come to after thinking the thing over carefully.

But to return to the block or check action which is so much to be preferred to the parry or guard as such. And here again one has to note yet one more advantage of the keeping close principle. You see, or you guess, or you have an instinct that your opponent is going to start a punch. Any sort of punch. It doesn't matter. All that you need see, guess or anticipate is which arm he is going to let go, and *that* part of your guess will be after all the easiest part. Then, instead of flinging up an arm across its path, which after all is a sheer waste both of time and of a useful weapon, just jab or push him sharply on the biceps or shoulder of the hitting limb. Even a push with the open glove will suffice. It is a matter of leverage this, and will effectively prevent the blow from coming through.

The selection of a jab or a push for the purpose will, or should, depend largely on circumstances and position. A push at the shoulder, if you propose to select the shoulder as the best place to be checked, is advisable, because you will not want to damage your knuckles by punching anything at all bony, or rather if you must hit a bony part, such as the jaw or temple, you will want it to be a place where a punch will be really effective, and a thump, however hard, on the shoulder isn't going to cause the other man any very violent pain, nor is it going to earn you any very vast amount of credit in the eyes of the referee.

On the other hand, if it seems to you that you can check the blow just as effectively by tapping the biceps, it isn't a bad plan to jab pretty hard. For a good sharp tap on the upper arm will not hurt your own knuckles and will very possibly do that arm quite a deal of damage. It won't put it out of action, of course, but a succession of such taps may, and probably will, considerably reduce its future effectiveness.

Don't forget, either, that these sudden checks, arriving just at moments when your opponent is preparing to disturb his balance, and has even to some extent commenced to disturb it, will inevitably send an unpleasant little jar rippling right through his system, both up to his brain and down to his heels, and in any case it isn't going to impress him that he is a fighting force.

Next, having checked the intended punch, don't draw back with the idea of basking in a glow of self-appreciation. Go ahead and take advantage of the further opening with which your own intelligent anticipation has just provided you. You are up close to your man. You have secured the interior lines, for the simple reason that since he has drawn back an arm in order to get a good wallop at you, you have been given a chance to step in between.

Well, you are there now and what are you going to do about it? Surely you are not going to step away and do nothing! Especially as you have already disturbed your man's balance and have not only got him more than a trifle rattled but have also placed yourself more than half-way to his chin, and have further deprived him of any possibility of interposing any protection thereto. It does not matter where you have checked. Any interposition, any tap, push or jolt either to his glove, wrist, forearm, biceps or shoulder, will have (or should have if you have applied any real checking force to your move) turned him the least fraction out of the straight. While if you haven't succeeded in making him wobble a trifle, you can only say that you have neglected to take full use of your opportunity.

The course to his jaw is a perfectly plain and straightforward one. All you have got to do is to clench your fist, swerve your body from the hips, in such a way as will add the full power of all your body weight and drive to the punch you are delivering. Add to this all the force you can derive from the drive of your leg muscles. In short, "pick your punch up from the floor" and pick it up all the way, even though your glove itself is only going to travel over a distance of 12 inches or less, and snap it right home as fast as you can.

Next, if possible-and it should be always possible-plant you other hand as a follow. (If your first and second punches have been good and true, you should be able to get home at least a couple more with either hand before the unfortunate fellow can recover-that is, of course, unless you have put him down earlier on, and thereby accorded him a chance of pulling himself round altogether while he is on the boards).

"Sounds easy, doesn't it?" Yes, I expected to hear you say that. Well, try it and see if it isn't nearly as easy as it sounds, provided all the details before, during and after work out all right for you, as they should do it you are half the man I take you to be, and will only bend your powerful mind to the task. Look at me (I hate having to ask you to do this, because it sounds as though I were in full agreement with all the promoters who bill me under such resounding titles. But then since I am trying to tell you what to do, I must quote from my own experience).

Blocking both an opponent's arms.

Note that he cannot possibly hit me with either fist and that I can hit him with either of my own and recapture my blocking position without running any risk unless he jumps right out of range.

So, though I didn't want to have to tell you to look at me, I've got to do it. You will have noted that I rarely allow any of my contests to go anywhere near the full distance, and you will also have noted that in every single instance-bar one-I have been giving away any number of points in weight, not to mention height, reach, bulk, years and everything else I could give away, except-well, I'll leave you to name the exceptions.

How have I done it? Well, I'm just trying to tell you how. And please remember that I am not now trying to write you a book on the complete science of the game of boxing, or even one on my own complete system of tactics and strategy, but simply just a few words on the twin subjects of hitting and stopping. In other words, a short outline of the plainest systems of attack and defence. There are numerous other sidelights on the game by the way, with which I may deal at a later date-but not within these covers. At least I hope not; though I must confess that I am finding it far from easy to avoid treading on other and forbidden ground (forbidden because I hope to get busy and to help out my meagre earnings that way on another occasion).

But to return to stopping. There is, if you have noticed, yet another method of stopping a punch, and even of stopping quite a number of punches, almost any sort of punch, in fact, and that is by keeping them stopped, before the

A right back-hander to the jaw.

This is the blow with which I coaxed Harry Brooks into exposing the jaw just before hooking with my left and winning a knock-out.
N.B. - The right was first crossed to miss intentionally and then back-handed.

other fellow can even think of starting them. It is perhaps the best of all methods, and I shouldn't be at all surprised to learn that it is vastly better than my own, because it must save one the labour of having to think out things beforehand. All the trouble of anticipation, forethought, insight and performance is avoided, and while one secures all the advantages of being able to hit straightaway from the stop, with all the full extra pull of having secured the interior lines, one has done it all without having been put to the worry of guessing what the other fellow is planning, and of consequently having to make sure of interposing one's push, tap, jab or parry. In other words, one relies simply and solely on one's sense of touch and on the telegraphic wires formed by the nerves of one's arms instead of having to call the wireless ones of the brain into service.

Watching other fellows do it, and experimenting with it myself, I have come to the conclusion that it must be an ideal method-one that I would like to play about with myself, if I were only a little bigger, heavier and consequently stronger. But then, as I always have to meet bigger, heavier and stronger men-I don't care to risk things. For I am pretty sure that it wouldn't *pay* me, though it ought to handsomely reward any and every practitioner who is only asked to tackle men of his own size and poundage.

It is Jim Driscoll's favourite. The method he always uses when he is meeting a man of his own weight. It must be admitted that he didn't play it against either Fred Welsh, Owen Moran, Spike Robson or Seaman Hayes, or at least that he only "kept touch" at intervals with Moran. But then Jim was up against a heavier man in Welsh and was in anything but the finest possible trim. He had been suffering from an abscess in his ear, and hadn't been able to enjoy a real good sleep for nearly a fortnight, while he had only just recovered from a bad attack of ptomaine poisoning when he met Moran.

Spike Robson, again, was Spike Robson. He is and was a man who never did anything like anyone else, and so I suppose Jim decided that it would be wisest to cut his coat according to his cloth. And as for Hayes, well, I guess that Driscoll just knew how to beat him by footwork, and didn't worry about trying to beat him by anything else. He didn't need to have to do so.

But to come back to the "keeping touch" method of stopping one's opponent's punches. One should possess at least fairly equal strength, or, to put things otherwise, fairly equal powers of resistance, since, although the "keep touch" artist may give and bend and allow the other man to apply the pressure, he must of necessity follow around, and so must not permit himself to be pushed clean out of the line.

The idea is as follows: One works in the usual style. Not necessarily by ducking or dodging, though these methods may, at times, be found useful as preliminaries, but by generally sparring up, until one has brought off a general half parry to both one's opponent's arms.

The idea is to establish "touch," and perhaps as good a method as any may be that of going into a clinch or half clinch and backing out there from with all four gloves in contact, your right with his left glove or forearm and your left with his right. (N.B.-That weird institution "the clean break" would absolutely bar any hope of getting into touch in the emergence from a clinch line).

Lastly, and this is of the first importance, be careful to secure touch *inside.* That is to say, with your arms inside your opponent's. This is essential, and if by any chance the positions are reversed, the only possible method, after a failure to get inside (and remember that the attempt should never be prolonged), is to jump clear and try again. That is to say, provided you do not feel sufficient confidence in your own powers to step right in close straight away and play the game recommended in the first chapter, etc.

Supposing that you have failed to secure touch; well you must just get along in the ordinary fashion until you can establish the connection as you want to establish it. Say that you have not fully accustomed yourself to the close-in, quick dodging backwards and forwards method of attack and defence, and say that you are so unfortunate as to be rather inexpert in the arts of ducking, dodging and slipping. Suppose that you are rather doubtful as to your ability to keep in close and rely on the tapping and checking of your opponent's punching arms. Supposing you are all these things, and these suppositions may be quite easily correct if you are better at the boxing than the fighting department of the game (these definitions are far from being the best, but they will have to serve).

You are, we have assumed, short in all these departments. Well, then, all that is left for you is to go right back, to use your feet and to play the long-range boxing game to the best of your abilities. But if you want to win, if you want to do any good at all at the game, for your own sake and for the game's, do try and do it intelligently. Think the thing out beforehand and play it as it should be played. Practise up beforehand, both at shadow boxing and in sparring practise.

You will find it absolutely necessary at times to interpose an arm on the parry or shield principle. Even this may be made useful at times, since you may be able to secure a good grasp on the interior lines when so doing, and may be able to step right in with a telling punch, provided always, when so doing, that you are not going to walk right in on top of a wallop from the hand which you have not parried.

But don't content yourself with just stopping the punch. You won't be doing much good that way unless you hit it off. You may, if you can, parry the punch with a glove and you may be able to turn the other fellow's fist right out of the line in so doing. But if you are taking the punch forearm to forearm, knock it away.

Suppose the punch is coming for your face, it is usually wisest to force it up; while if it is aimed for your body, it is generally advisable to push it down. There is, of course, always a risk of one getting fouled when one pushes these body blows down, and it may perhaps be an open question as to whether one is really entitled to the decision in such circumstances, seeing that one has been a contributory; but since every boxer who has any common sense at all will always be wise enough to wear a cup, the risk is practically negligible.

But better than the parry or buckler defence of the arm, better than either the push down or the knock up or aside, made from the inside position, as practically all parries are, it will be found vastly more profitable to make use of your feet, to get back, or sway back before the attack and to the punch downwards from the outside.

It doesn't really matter whether the blow be a straight delivery, a hook or a swing in this case.

In either or each of these instances your opponent must have got perilously close to the verge of his balancing powers by the mere action of lashing out. Your withdrawal, either on your feet or by the sway of your body, will have brought him right up to the brink of overbalancing, and not impossibly even past the brink, simply because he has missed and is probably following his punch, especially if the said punch was intended to be a hard one.

It will consequently require but a very slight tap on his extended arm to bring him stumbling forward. His feet will go astray, and at least a second or so must elapse before he can properly recover his position and correct balance. And you surely will not want more than a second or two in which to deliver a seriously telling and perhaps a winning punch.

But to get back to the "keeping touch" system of defence. We have made a long digression, but there was method to it, even though I may have failed to make the method quite as clear as I should have liked.

All the other modes of defence are inferior to this one, which not only cannot be improved on for out-fighting, but which is absolutely essential to successful in-fighting, provided the other fellow insists on fighting you close up, with head, elbows and wrist punches going, and you are not (as I hope you are not) anxious to protect yourself on the clutching, wrestling and roughing American lines. If you do not want to haul and tug to get your arms free, you must be content to interpose your forearms as a barrier. The other fellow can then hook and jab for all he is worth, but if you have only worked both your arms inside, he will find it impossible either to rest his weight on you or to pull his arms back out of touch with yours.

You will then be relieved of the necessity for either watching his movements or for guessing at his intentions. You will be able to divine his intentions by the sense of touch, and will thus have secured the three strongest advantages it is possible to hold in any boxing contest.

Firstly, you are in a position to know all that your opponent is meditating. Secondly, you are so placed that he cannot possibly hit you without your permission, either voluntary or involuntary. You have the inside lines and really, unless you are the veriest of novices, you should be able to follow his arms wherever they travel, unless he sees fit to disengage by a big and sudden leap backwards.

He cannot rush you, because you can meet him as he comes forward. He cannot throw himself on you, because you can pound away at his body, the moment his arms slide so far forward that you no longer need worry about keeping touch, until they have returned to a position from which they may dispossess you of the interior lines, and all the time you will be retaining a position from which you can either hook, uppercut or jab him at will. Some of you may quite possibly recall the Driscoll-Poesy contest, and how powerless the Frenchman was to inflict injury against Driscoll's interior lines of defence. Poesy strove for all he was worth to disengage his arms. Jim never held once, and was scarcely even closer than full arm's length from his opponent, and yet he jabbed and punched the Frenchman at will.

It is true that Poesy got free at times. The gong which closured the rounds enabled him to get away every three minutes, and Jim was not able to secure the desired situation at once. The Frenchman was practically at his wits end before the end came. He had to jump back and then to make a final bold bid for victory by launching himself furiously at Driscoll, and therein he delivered himself right into Jim's hands.

Driscoll had only to step back, sway out of the way of Poesy's furious lunge, knock his arm aside and then cross him on the chin. That blow practically finished the Frenchman. It is true that Jim had to hit him twice more, but the affair was all over in a couple more seconds.

ON DAMAGED HANDS
& BACKHAND PUNCHES

Chapter Four
On Damaged Hands and Backhanded Punches

The first of the above seems to be fairly prevalent these days, and would seem to afflict boxers more than they ever did since the introduction of bandages and the boxing gloves. I have had my experience of them myself, and I must confess that they are about the last things anyone wants to collect. Yet I still continue to win in spite of them, and in spite of the fact that I have not been able to claim a really sound pair of hands any time during the past two years.

It hasn't been easy to get along, and I can remember contests on which I have entered with one hand so badly out of commission that I was really afraid to use it for even the gentlest punch. That was my right, by the way, which had been badly burnt, in addition to being knocked up round the knuckles and wrist joint. There was also a bone up in the back, but I am fairly well used to that state of things. Really and truly, I couldn't, I dared not use that hand at all. It would have hurt me too much, and besides I doubt whether I could have delivered any punch with it which would have been of the slightest use.

Then my left wasn't in very much better case. Two of the knuckles were badly swollen and almost out of joint, while the back of the hand was badly swollen. But I had to win. My opponent was a really careful boy, one of the best I had ever met, and he was also some 8 or 9lbs. heavier.

I had only my left to rely on, though I could use my right for defensive purposes. The situation looked a bit awkward, so I decided to employ my right as usefully as I could. Not to hit with, but to miss with. For there is great virtue in a missed punch, if you only know how to turn the trick.

Harry Brooks may have heard that my hands were in a bad way, but he could not *know* how bad they were, and might be inclined to suspect that the rumours as to their condition had been grossly exaggerated. I knew that he wasn't likely to give me openings for knock-out punches if he noted that I was only able to use my left. So I tapped away with the left, just as though I were trying to force an opening for my right.

I did not work in as close as I usually do. Firstly, because I could not rely on my right hand for stopping purposes in the event of my getting into trouble, and also because, as I wasn't going to use it for any effective purpose, I was naturally anxious to allow myself some space in which to miss. Besides, I wanted Harry to open out so that I could get a chance of doing something really effective with my left.

I crossed my right two or three times, and I hooked with it more than once; but I was always careful to miss connection, just as I was always careful to avoid missing by any too wide a margin. And finally, in order to disabuse Harry's mind of any idea which might creep into it, to the effect that I was purposely missing with it, I set my teeth and back-handed him two or three times. They weren't exactly punches, but they were pretty hard flaps, and as they were landed with knuckles they were not only perfectly legitimate, but also just about as much as I could bear. But they served their purpose. They satisfied Brooks that my right hand was in thorough working order, and whenever I slipped it across after that he was most careful to dodge it. He even drew back once or twice when I showed it to him, and I was glad of this, because he was pressing me pretty hard at the time.

In fact, he grew so respectful of my damaged right, which I really should not have cared to risk at all, as to actually present me with no less than three openings. That is to say, he was in such a hurry to dodge the right that I was able to hook him with my left on three out of the seven or eight times on which he went to the boards before he was counted out, all the openings for which came through my right hand displays. From which you will see that a right which you cannot use may be almost as useful as one which you can.

As to the back-hand punch, which has grown considerably in popularity among professional boxers of late, I may say that this can be employed as a most respectable punch when sent to the chin. For instance, one may hook or cross a right which one isn't absolutely certain will land direct. In that case it may pay well to send it along as an intentional miss, one which just grazes the chin, and *then*, as the other fellow's face comes forward, it can be flicked back sharply with a distinctly jarring effect.

I have known a man to score a knock-down with it, though hardly ever a knock out. Yet the K.O. may follow on all the same, for the backhander will, or may, turn the face around, and may, as already stated, have given a preliminary jar which may be forwarded to the brain with temporarily stunning effect, if sharply and smartly followed up by a well-hooked left to the right place.

ADDENDUM

Addendum
Contents

The Secret Of My Success
Jimmy Wilde

It is very gratifying, no doubt, but it is nevertheless a little wearying, when one has to open one's daily paper in a gingerly fashion, because one is afraid that one may have had a new label pasted on to one overnight. The flattery is very well meant, of course, but then it is always liable to be double-edged.

Can I carry the corn?

I believe that I was so constituted by Nature as to be able to carry a quite respectable load of corn, but then we have all heard about the last straw which broke the camel's back, and I am always a little nervous lest I may wake up one morning to discover that none of my hats would fit me. Hitherto I have been fortunately able to brace myself up with the recollection that sooner or later we shall all have to meet our masters, and that I cannot hope to escape the general fate myself. But when I do have to taste defeat, I shall at least have the consolation of knowing that I shall be able to boast that my list of victories is considerably longer than that of my defeats. I believe that no matter how long I live nor how many years I stay in the ring, I shall always be able to say that. For, although I only reached my twenty-second birthday last May, I have already chalked up some 200 wins, and cannot recall a single defeat or even a single split decision.

Why did someone not present me with a Scrap Book?

No, I am afraid I could not possibly give a complete list of my contests, nor even of half of them, because when I started out to box for money it never occurred to me that I should ever become important enough to make the list a matter of importance to anyone else. So I never jotted them down. Somebody told me that I ought to keep the clippings, or to at least scribble down the names of the men I met, with the results, dates, and places, and I started to do this about July, 1911, and since then I have kept a record of my last 90-odd ring battles, which works out at an average of 30 a year, though I have at times fought three times per week. Not always, of course, because even the professional boxer has to rest up at times, especially when his hands start to go to pieces as badly as mine have during the last six months or so.

Where my punch came from and how

"But how do you do it, Jimmy?" they come round and ask. "Where do you get your punch from?"

Well, I'm blest if I know. The thing that has puzzled me most is why the other fellows don't do it as well. It is surely easy enough. You have only to watch your opponent carefully, to look keenly at his eye, and to generally keep your senses alert, and then you can usually be perfectly certain beforehand of everything, or at all events of most of the things that he is going to do.

I am often asked how it is that I manage to avoid getting punched by some of the much heavier men that I meet. I can't say, unless it is because I usually manage to get my punch in first. You see I don't waste either my breath or my strength by running around. As far as I can see, a boxer can be quite as safe and well protected as he is close up to his opponent as he can possibly be when he is trying to run away from him. Safer, in fact, because he can keep himself in perfect poise and readiness, if he isn't wasting his thoughts or his energies in endeavouring to widen the distance the other fellow's punches will have to travel.

Keep cool and you won't miss

Besides, so long as one keeps cool and collected, one is less liable to miss when one hits out. Of course, one misses at times, both when one intends to miss and when one has meant to get there, but as a rule one should be careful to miss as seldom as possible. Misses encourage one's opponents and disturb one's own chain of thought.

Don't forget this, either way, because you can make the miss very useful at times. Say that you are up against a man who is boxing very cautiously, and who refuses to leave you any more openings that he can help. Well, then, don't be in any too great a hurry to take a too heavy advantage of such openings as may come along in the early stages.

The advantages of missing judiciously

Let fly a punch or so, of course, but be careful to miss. Make the punches look real not only to your opponent, but also to the spectators, because this will encourage him, and make him believe that you are not nearly so formidable as he has been led to imagine. He will then, in all probability, lash out at you with all his force, or at all events with a good deal of it, and every time he does that he is going to give you a chance to cross or to hook him.

He may hit you, you say. Well, there is of course always that risk to take, but then if you are going to make up your mind that you are never going to run any risks, you may just as well decide that you are never going to make any great headway in the boxing game. For unless your opponent stands a fairly sound chance of winning, the match will be a very poor attraction from the gate-money point of view.

The training of eye and instinct

Besides, if you have really trained your eye correctly and possess a real instinct for the game, you ought to be fairly certain when your opponent is going to punch, which fist he is going to punch with, and also the way it is coming. You can even, to a large extent, make sure on all these points by presenting him with the proper sort of opening to hit through.

You can then either check his punch by pushing against his biceps, avoid it by ducking or drawing back at the right moment, or, if you must, stop it by interposing your forearm or glove as a guard. This last, however, only as a final resource, because it is a waste both of time and strength. A sway back, remember, will always increase the force of your return punch.

Don't forget the sting

And, by the way, when you are punching either as a lead or as a counter, be careful to make sure that your punch will carry plenty of sting behind it.

Training in a narrow coal seam

How can one develop a punch? That is another question I often have fired at me. Well, I don't know if I ever worried about developing one. I found that I had one when I first commenced to make use of my fists among my fellow pit-boys. Perhaps those hitting muscles got developed by my work in the low galleries where I used to lie on my side and pick at the coal-seam. The gallery wasn't much thicker than I am myself, and I could only just manage to squeeze myself in when I crawled. I have heard it said and seen it written that work of this character tends to make the worker muscle-bound, but I cannot say that this has been my experience.

The other fellow will make you a present of the power

No; I think, after all, that the real force of a punch comes chiefly from the pace at which the recipient meets it. I have seen it stated that the secret of my success is my wonderful judgement of distance and almost "uncannily clever footwork." It may be so, but I cannot say that I ever fancied that I had been miraculously endowed in either direction. Such judgement of distance and such footwork ability as I may possess "just growed," like Topsy. I suppose I did have some knack in both directions, but the rest was all observation, practice, and a sincere idea to preserve my head on my shoulders for as long as I was able.

I had to hit out or go under

When I started with the boxing booth I used to meet boys and men who were both much bigger and heavier than myself, and I was soon able to realise that unless I discouraged them very speedily I might quite easily be put out of the business myself. So I took special pains to hit them first, whenever I saw them start a punch or guessed that they were going to start one, and as they used to come forward with their wallops, I found that my punches (when they met them half-way) were much more effective than I had believed they could be.

My hardest battles

Which was my stiffest contest? Well, that isn't such a very easy question to answer, but I believe that Young Dando and Alf Mansfield have given me more trouble than any of the others. I met Dando three times, as I dare say you remember, over fifteen rounds at Tonypandy, and over twenty rounds at Cardiff, when I won on points each time, and again at Merthyr, when I won on a foul in the tenth round.

Alf Mansfield also took me through twenty rounds at Leeds, and said afterwards that he wasn't satisfied with himself. I hear that he has been saving himself up for September 29th at the New Edgware Road Stadium*. Well, I am getting into good shape as well, so we ought both to enjoy ourselves, and I hope you will as well.

Jimmy Wilde

* (Wilde went on to beat Alf Mansfield in the 10th round in this fight)

My Greatest Battle
Jimmy Wilde

Which was the greatest victory I ever achieved? Frequently this question has been fired at me. I have never before troubled to supply the answer. For you must remember that since I was a wisp of a lad of sixteen I have fought over 500 battles in the ring, never meeting a rival of my own weight, 6st. 4lb., but always tackling bantams, feathers, lights and even welter-weights.

Now that I can reflect upon my hectic career I can say definitely that my greatest winning fight was against the American bantam champion, Joe Lynch, for a purse of £2,400 at the old National Sporting Club at Covent Garden in 1919. What a wonderful night that was! The small theatre - it did not accommodate more than 1,500 spectators - was packed together with Britain's most distinguished sportsmen, including "The Prince". There was an atmosphere in that historic and exclusive building that will never be captured again.

Lynch was reared in the Irish quarter of New York. A handsome sandy -complexioned boy he was, magnificently built, with blue speedwell eyes and a punch that was charged with dynamite. I can see him now, shy and disarming, when the Prince of Wales stepped into the ring to shake hands with us. And behind him stood Eddie McGoorty, greatest of American middle-weights, the shrewd boxer who first told me to take notice of a young fellow coming along named Jack Dempsey!

Lynch was no stranger to me. I had outpointed him over three rounds in the Inter-Allied Tournament at the end of the War at the Royal Albert Hall. But he seemed a formidable giant this time as I glanced at his well-trained body. The thought raced through my mind: "He's going to give me a lot of trouble. He's a tough fellow. But I shall beat him."

And beat him I did, but it was a tremendous struggle for fifteen pulsating rounds. A fight with the fortunes fluctuating. The Americans were sure that Lynch had won. Several prominent members said they were sure Lynch could have won had he not been so apprehensive throughout the contest of my knockout punch. And his chief second, McGoorty, kept whispering and imploring Lynch to be careful of my right-hand punch. I could hear the advice given to Lynch in my own corner! But the late James White was full of glee, and he chuckled and laughed and shouted in my corner: "You're winning easily, Jimmy!" I knew this myself without being told by excited Jimmy White.

Lynch certainly fought a marvellous fight. He looked twice as big as I did, with his determined face and powerful shoulders. It often has been said that he could have beaten me, because he stood nearly six inches taller! But Lynch crouched exceedingly low throughout the fight. This was a curious change in his stance, because hitherto he had always stood upright and fought exactly in a style similar to Jim Driscoll.

There was never a dull moment, although it is significant that Lynch - twice my size as I have said-was warned at least a dozen times for holding and as many times for "laying on". It was in the first round the Irish-American exposed his most obvious weakness. I had scored freely with right upper-cuts, straight lefts and body blows, and Lynch began boxing on the defensive. He started ducking as low as any boxer could possibly do. And I knew then I had the fight in my pocket. I was surprised that the American bantam champion was consciously showing inferior methods. So I decided to take no risks and win the match on points.

Lynch was always smart with his leads and his bobbing and weaving. He even thumped me pretty solidly about the ribs. Every round contested was a battle of wits. I had never before had to manoeuvre so much in a fight.

From the moment we shook hands I knew that Lynch was going to prove troublesome. He crouched low, and then when I shot out a lead, would bob up and deliver a heavy blow with a left hook. I did not over exert myself. Why should I? Lynch was as strong as a bull terrier, and I had planned to beat him on points. So we feinted and lunged at each other, Lynch seemingly afraid to take any risks. I began to get going in the second round and found that I could break through his crafty defence fairly easily.

But Lynch refused to take part in an open fight. Acting on the advice of Eddie McGoorty, Lynch tried occasional left hooks to my jaw, but his principal object was to nail me with heavy blows on the body. I was completely aware of his intentions, and to prevent him from doing me any serious damage I kept up a persistent attack with snappy left and right hand punches. These generally landed first and kept Joe at bay, thus proving that attack is the finest form of defence.

I kept scoring points so frequently that at the end of every round I knew I was ahead on points. I have since been told by sportsmen who sat at the ringside that they could not understand why Lynch did not make a bold effort to win with a knockout! Well, my answer to this query is: Nobody better than Lynch understood the risk he would be taking. *Because without boasting* I can say that my punch was much harder than Lynch's. My object was to prevent him from putting me on the canvas. I was quite content to know that he was unable to do this, so I kept fiercely attacking from the start to the finish. I can honestly declare that at no period during these sizzling fifteen rounds did I feel in any danger of meeting with defeat.

It was not until the twelfth round that Lynch really caught me. Then he landed a blow on my chin that shook me for a moment. But I quickly recovered and realised that I must be wary. Lynch knew then that the only way to make certain of victory was with a knockout blow. How desperately he tried to perform the trick. Yet he failed. And there was a hush in his corner every time he sat on his stool between rounds for a minute's rest and to listen to the advice of his chief second, McGoorty.

Lynch delayed his real aggressive action until the last four rounds. Then he was surprised to find that my defence was as good as my attack. I know that we must have exchanged hundreds of punches during those fifteen rounds. Yet although Lynch cracked me on the chin or thumped me on the body on no single occasion was I in the least distressed. I could have gone on for 50 rounds. Nobody present expected Lynch to tire. His massive frame indicated strength and stamina, besides; he was nearly a couple of stones heavier than I was.

Joe Lynch was a gentlemanly type, and one of the best sportsmen I've met. We chatted in the National Sporting Club Lounge afterwards, when he said to me: "I never believed a little fellow like you could last fifteen rounds with me. You are more than a marvel-you are a miracle!" It was a testimonial to our skill when I say that neither of us showed any marks after we had fought one of the most discussed ring battles of the century.

But I am convinced that Lynch was as brilliant as the master craftsman, Pete Herman, the Italian who beat me at the Albert Hall, and whom I met afterwards in New Orleans, a tragic figure, blinded but cheerful. I shall pay Herman the compliment of acknowledging that he was too good for me. He was 8st. 9lb. and I was 6st. 7lb. But the night I beat Lynch I was at the peak of my form, and it was well for me that I was. The slightest mistake on my part would have been fatal. But as I remember that battle I cannot recall any result during my career which pleased me as much as when I beat America's best bantam.

Jimmy Wilde

How Wilde Developed His Skill

Jim Driscoll
(British Featherweight Champion)

Something like seven years ago Mr. Teddy Lewis, of Pontypridd, came to me at a sports meeting in his town, and said he wanted me to go to a contest that night, at the Millfield Club, as he had "a little boy" there, who ought to make a good 'un. I went, and for the first time set my eyes upon Jimmy Wilde. If he is small now, he was then a mere speck, so to speak, and in what was styled, out of courtesy, as a four-rounds exhibition he conceded about half a stone to his rival, and probably received about "ten bob" as his end of the purse. My conclusions were that he was a game little boy, but had a lot to learn. I told Lewis so, and added that Wilde would be too small to get on in the profession, because we had no championships for lads of his weight. At that time, you must remember, he was only about 5st, and to me he looked as though he never would grow any bigger. Later on Mr. Lewis had him fixed up for a 10 rounds contest at Tonypandy, and he asked me if I would have him down with me. I consented, and when he came I 'nursed' him for his test, and allowed him to box with some of my sparring partners - Salem Sullivan, Badger Brien and Joe Johns - three very useful lads. I told Wilde to follow me closely in all I did. If he found anything good in what I did, he was to try it, and if he saw me doing something which did not appeal to him, then he need not attempt it, or, at least, he should try to find a way to beat it. Well, with his natural gift for fighting and his good brain, Wilde did not require to be told twice before he grasped an idea and put it into execution.

I found him improving daily when I sparred with him, and now he knows the game from A to Z. If I were asked to give reasons for his wonderful success, I should say it is due to the quick way in which his brain works. It certainly travels faster than that of the majority of boxers. He sees the opening and takes advantage of it quickly, whilst he also knows if he does anything wrong, so that he is able to recover himself immediately.

Add to this Wilde's unnatural strength-which is phenomenal in a man of his weight-and bearing in mind also his sound knowledge of the game, you can then see what pulls him through many trying contests. This was proved in his match with Joe Lynch. It was simply Wilde's knowledge and his gameness that kept him on his feet when Lynch had him practically beaten. I think it was in the twelfth or thirteenth round that this occurred. Wilde was not having things his own way, but he used his head, and bluffed and fought Lynch out of it. His hitting power, which has long astonished the medical profession as well as followers of boxing, comes naturally with his strength and his speed. Besides he punches properly, so with his speed he is bound to hit hard. It is like a racehorse kicking. A racehorse can do as much damage with its kick as a heavy carthorse entirely owing to the speed of the kick. Wilde, again, always works a man into position to hit with either hand, and that is where he uses his ring craft.

It is some feat to make an opponent go into the position you are engineering. Someone at Cardiff last week asked me what I considered to be Wilde's hardest contest. I should say it was his match with Dai Chips at Tonypandy, which Mr. Chas. Barnett refereed. On that occasion Jimmy was giving away 2st. to one of our best Welsh lads, and, bear this in mind, they were boxing in a 12ft. ring with scarcely room to swing a cat. For a boy about 5½ st. to give away 2st. was nothing short of marvellous, and remember, he was only a youngster at the game.

That indeed was one of his best displays, for although the people of England had not up to that time seen much of Chips, we in Wales knew he was a good man. I seconded Wilde that night, and I may say that I acted in a similar capacity for all his important battles, except the time he lost to Tancy Lee; up to the time I went to France I was always in his corner.

A funny thing occurred when I was training to meet Poesy in 1912. Mr. Bettinson, Mr. Frank Bradley, and I believe, the late Mr. George Dunning, came down to see me train, and I told them I would show them the makings of three champions - Percy Jones, Llew Edwards, and Jimmy Wilde. Not one of the trio was known at the time, yet all three won Lonsdale belts. After I had boxed the three I asked Mr. Bettinson his opinion, and he replied that Jones and Edwards were fairish lads, but he thought Wilde was too small altogether to ever come to the top. I noticed afterwards, however, that Mr. Bradley did mention that "he saw the makings of three champions."

Well the three became champions, and Wilde has come out practically on his own. It was my opinion then that he would be the best of the three, but I never thought he would be able to give class men like Lee and Conn nearly two stone, though I felt he would give half a stone and a beating to anyone in England.

They say Wilde has lost his punch. I don't think so, because every time he had a 'fight' he made Lynch stop first, and he must be hitting hard to make Lynch stop and hold. If Wilde lost his punch then, by the look of things, he found it again in his contest with Jimmy Buck! People imagine a man has lost his punch merely because he doesn't knock his men out, but some opponents are different from others. They don't take a punch because they know as much about boxing as those delivering the punch, and besides they do not show the effect of it. But, after all, the chief factor in Wilde's wonderful success is his brain and the use he makes of it.

Jim Driscoll

Tales of the Tylorstown Terror
Charles Barnett

"Well, Mr. Bottomley, I didn't see you at Ascot today!"

This remark, made by none other than Jimmy Wilde at Olympia on the night of the Beckett and Goddard match, attracted my attention, and I could not help feeling how kindly the world had dealt with the wonderful little Welshman, in whose battles I have officiated as referee on over fifty occasions.

When I first met Wilde he had not taken to boxing as a profession. He was just a little collier-boy, and a poor specimen at that. His pale face and skinny body were in those days referred to more from pity than wonder, and old Jack Skarratt, the quaint booth-proprietor, was often rebuked for daring to allow "the poor boy" to stand up against burly colliers in a 12ft. ring.

You have all read that Jimmy Wilde was at first rejected by a medical board because of a weak leg. Well, there was every reason for it, as whilst in his teens Wilde met with an accident in the pit that threatened to end in amputation of one of his limbs. He was caught by a haulage-rope underground, and his leg was so frightfully lacerated that for just a year he was able only to hobble about on crutches.

At that time the present world's champion knew nothing about boxing other than to be able to "take his own part". He had, it is true, emerged successfully from a street-fight with an Italian ice-cream boy, but there was nothing to distinguish him from any other pit-boy, save, perhaps, his puny figure.

Wilde lived in lodgings when he met with the accident in the pit, and prior to that he and a little sister were the support of his mother and the family, the father having also been injured in the mine. In the early hours of each day the boy and girl had to collect coal from the Tylorstown tips, whilst in the evening they pounded sandstone, it being a common practice in Wales to sprinkle sand on the floors after they had been scrubbed. Little Jimmy and his sister were sent round the streets to sell this, and by the coppers from these sales the wolf was kept from the door. But there came a time when Master Wilde was forced to earn a living for himself. He went into lodgings, and secured work as a collier-boy in the Tylorstown collieries, which later, by the way, passed under the control of the late Lord Rhondda, himself a former light-weight champion of Cambridge.

Young Wilde's days of adversity had, however not yet ended. As mentioned, he was caught by a wire-rope, and for a long time was at death's door. Indeed, the pluck which has characterised his ring battles undoubtedly had a lot to do with his recovery, and to be in lodgings at such a critical period was only one of his troubles. His landlady was quite willing and good-hearted enough to support him, but as time went on and the lad was still on crutches, she hinted that her financial position made it imperative that something should be done.

Then came the turning-point in the lad's career-a turning point that has brought him wealth, fame, and happiness. Jimmy told me the whole story in his own quiet way, and from other sources also I know it to be true. "I restarted work," said Jimmy, "and then-I got married. And I don't mind telling you now," he added, as an afterthought, "that I borrowed the suit for the wedding from the pack man."

By a curious coincidence, Miss Davies, the plump young woman who became Mrs. Jimmy Wilde, is the daughter of an old-time local champion boxer, but this, the greatest match ever made by Wilde, was not due to hero-worship, as Jimmy up to that time had not been in a ring. It was clearly a love-match. In later years I could not help noticing, however, that the most energetic of Wilde's towel slingers was Dai Davies, the old knuckle-fighter, Wilde's father-in-law.

It was about this time that old Jack Skarratt found Wilde. Skarratt is known in every village in South Wales. At each fair he is to be found outside his booth gesticulating wildly, slashing with a stick, and generally working up excitement in his own inimitable way. He invites all and sundry to have the gloves on with champions inside, "And the price to-night, gen'elmen, is sixpence!"

One evening the appeal, "Walk up! Walk up!" by old Skarratt met with a strange reply. A weak-looking collier youth - a human hairpin - went inside the booth and agreed to meet another collier. The latter, without exaggeration, was twice as big as the challenger, who, needless to explain, was Wilde, but even in those days Jimmy never looked at the size of an opponent.

I have been in the same ring with Jimmy Wilde on probably forty occasions, and I still wonder how he is alive to tell the tale. It was a 12ft. affair, the sort of place you would say you could not swing a cat in, yet from such cramped quarters, with no room for footwork, Wilde never failed to emerge successfully. I have seen him stagger from rope to rope, I have watched men stones heavier than himself rush him from one side to the other like a fly, and I have heard people cry "Shame! Stop it!" out of sheer pity for the frail little figure who was expecting to receive nothing more than fair-play from me.

And what happened? Jimmy in nearly every case knocked his man out! It was so on his first experience of Skarratt's ring, and it followed with monotonous regularity.

"Man alive!" declared Skarratt to me not so long ago. "He knocked out six navies one after the other for me. He's -he's -" And words failed even Jack Skarratt!

I have no desire to take all the glory for introducing Wilde to the outside world. Immense credit must be given to his manager, Teddy Lewis, who "picked him up" from Skarratt, but it was the old showman who first brought Wilde to my notice.

I have it from Wilde himself that Skarratt gave him five shillings for beating that burly collier, and in those days five shillings was great wealth to the champion. Wilde boxed often afterwards for similar sums, but when he linked himself up to Teddy Lewis, a business-like basis was established, and I have recollections of an agreement with Skarratt to pay Wilde eight pounds a match. Just fancy the change - five shillings to eight pounds!

It was in those days that I became rather closely connected with Wilde's career. As a sporting editor of the Cardiff "Evening Express," it often fell to my lot to referee side-stake matches in strange places, and Jimmy Wilde and his collier friends and rivals provided me with all the excitement I needed.

Old Skarratt possessed scanty accommodation in the shape of a dressing-tent, yet boxers who have fought each other to the last bell occupied places side by side in this tent after the bout, and I honestly say I have never seen or heard a quarrel as they dressed.

But when I have taken up my position in the ring with a sea of surging faces around me, I have marvelled at the change. Wilde, even in those days, used to pack the marquee, and the excitement he created was tremendous.

As a matter of fact, the Welsh collier is the greatest sport on earth. He can shout with the best, but give him a fair run for his money and he is satisfied. The Jimmy Wilde series of matches never gave me the slightest anxiety, and the crowd being apparently satisfied with my decisions, I became a regular fixture at the shows.

In this way I grew accustomed to the style of Wilde, and I recognized that in him we had a champion of champions-a freak and a marvel combined. About this time Sergeant Jim Driscoll was on the lookout for sparring-partners, and as Wilde was to box Kid Fitzpatrick at Cardiff Stadium, a sort of double event was arranged. Now, as all the world knows, Driscoll was, and is still, a master of the noble art, and what Wilde did not know, the featherweight champion taught him. Driscoll treated Wilde as a 'joke'. If any man came to

Driscoll and boasted he could box, Wilde was the test.

Soon Wilde's deeds began to be talked about, and all refused to accept the tales until they had seen him at work for themselves. When they were told by Driscoll that "the boy" was not only married, but a father, they were still more amazed.

Today Wilde is the father of two boys. The elder, James, is chiefly remarkable for his studious ways, and for the possession of a surprising knowledge of his father's ring tricks. The younger of the two was named Verdun, in honour of France's glorious stand, and Mrs. Wilde informed me some little time after he was born that he already had more to say than his father!

Wilde's first appearance at the N.S.C. was in an exhibition with Joe Wilson on the night of the Driscoll v. Poesy contest, but when the club patrons saw Wilde entering the ring during what was regarded as an interval, the majority walked out of the theatre to the bar! Prior to that night I had tried to persuade Mr. Bettinson to put Wilde on for a real bout, but when I said he only weighed 6st. 10lbs., it was "napoo." Lord Lonsdale, who listened to my argument, remarked, "Ah, but you must try and breed some heavyweights!" I believe his lordship likes to see Wilde better than any of the big men now.

The visit of Wilde to the N.S.C. was preceded by a visit to the Ring in Blackfriars Road, and here Wilde tackled a nephew of Matt Wells. In this connection I can tell a funny story. Fred Delaney was in the programme, and he was very much concerned about catching a train to Bradford, so as Wilde seemed in no hurry to take off his Welsh flannel-shirt to get ready for the fray Delaney grew rather annoyed.

"Oh, you" catch your train all right," said Wilde, as he sauntered towards the arena. Inside five minutes he was back, and this fairly aroused Delaney.

"Are you going on?" he asked.

"I've been on," drawled Wilde. "Knocked him out first round!"

Through the instrumentality of Teddy Lewis, the Tylorstown Terror one day found himself matched to appear at Liverpool Stadium, and his road to prosperity was open. The time came when Wilde was not asked to put on a boxing-glove for less than £50, excepting for charity. Nowadays that is a fleabite.

I have seen it stated "on authority" that Wilde received £500 for beating the Zulu Kid. I would be delighted to receive the amount paid to him above that. It is not fair to give away figures, but Wilde holds the world's record for income as a flyweight.

I have been asked, "What does he do with all his money?" That natural question can be answered, with additional praise for Wilde. He does not drink, he does not smoke; but an outlet for his vast earnings has been found in judicious investment. The house Wilde lives in has been bought and paid for long ago, and, acting on the advice of a well-to-do tradesman - who, by the way, is to accompany Wilde to America - he had been able to add to his income.

I am not concerned with the money-making powers of Wilde, but it is a real pleasure to be able to record that he does not squander his wealth. The old-time pugilist generally got rid of his money in quick time; but Wilde has had a hard time, and knows the value of it.

One of his most remarkable performances took place during the National Railway strike of 1912. Wilde, at that time, was still unknown outside South Wales, although I tried to convince lots of sporting people that the lad was a future champion. Skarratt was his "universal provider." It so happened that the quaint old showman was at Caerphilly Fair, and he sent word to Wilde that he could have thirty shillings to box a local named Roberts. What reply could Jimmy give? He was still digging a precarious living in the coal-mine, and the birth of a son and heir added to the needs of the moment, so Jimmy resolved to accept. But to get to Caerphilly from Tylorstown he had to cover some ground, which included a walk over a mountain. This, however, did not prevent him from going on with the bout, and he defeated his opponent in three rounds.

Teddy Lewis, Wilde's manager, was firmly of opinion a year or so ago that Wilde would put on a little weight whilst in the ranks. If Mr. Lewis' prophecy came true, then we might have seen Wilde challenging middle-weights!

In this connection, I can tell a story to illustrate Wilde's lack of fear. When Billy Ames ran shows in Cardiff, one of his top-of-the-bill items was a match between Pat O'Keefe and Marthuin, a French heavy-weight.

We had been led to expect much from our ally. He was described as a likely "white hope," but the display, without exaggeration, was the tamest seen in Wales, as Marthuin was a poor sample of a boxer. The rounds were watched for a long time in a silence which betrayed disgust, but a loud and clever incitation of a man snoring set the crowd roaring.

When they grew silent again a voice from the roof suddenly urged the pair to "fight," and it was discovered that even a youngster who had accomplished the feat of securing a free but perilous seat had become annoyed at the exhibition.

Jimmy Wilde, Ted Lewis, and myself followed the proceedings with a bored feeling, and eventually Wilde turned to us, and in an earnest tone said: "I believe I could beat the two of them!" There was an absolute lack of what is termed "swank" in the remark. It was a studied and convinced opinion of a wizard who is unabashed by the size of his opponents. Some people will be inclined to ridicule the idea; but as one who has constantly been in Wilde's company, I can honestly say the remark was spoken with conviction.

Doesn't talk boxing

Indeed Wilde seldom talks about boxing. He is, even to myself, a mystery in that respect. I organized a charity show at Barry for the Tuesday night before he met the Zulu Kid, and Wilde and Sergeant-major Billy Wells gave exhibitions there. They met in a dressing-room, and, after cordial greetings, Wells asked Wilde what he thought of his chance against the Zulu Kid.

"I haven't seen him," replied Jimmy nonchalantly; "but," he added, "they do tell me he comes at you like this!" - and Wilde imitated piston-rod punches.

The one subject on which Wilde will literally talk you to death is golf. He kept on telling everyone he met, after his contest with the American, that J.H Taylor, the golf champion, was at the Stadium. Strange though it may seem, he lives for golf, and to that boxing is a mere side-show. Wilde has won the championship of the Mid-Rhondda Golf Club, and the trophy he thus gained is cherished far more than all the others. Many times I have tried to draw him on the subject of boxing, and on each occasion he has quickly changed the conversation to "handicap terms" on the Mid-Rhondda course.

On one occasion we were travelling to London together, when the door in the corridor side of the train was opened and an officer stepped in. "Which of you is Jimmy Wilde?" he asked courteously. I at once motioned in the direction of my companion. With an apology for intruding, the officer explained that he was a surgeon, and was returning to France; but, having heard in the dining-car that Jimmy Wilde was aboard, he could not resist the desire to meet him. Inside two minutes Wilde was talking golf to him!

Wilde vs. Sid Smith

Wilde's programme for that particular day will further illustrate this amazing air of indifference. He was due to meet Sid Smith for the third time, the venue being Hoxton Baths, and he left Tylorstown at eight a.m., being joined at Pontypridd by his manager, and at Cardiff by myself. Hardly had we entered the through train when Wilde began complaining that he was hungry, and when told that lunch would not be put on in the dining car until noon, he was in absolute misery. Naturally, we chaffed him, but we failed to make him smile. Eventually twelve o'clock came, and Wilde was among the first at the tables. Mr. Lewis and I agreed we "could do with a good feed," and we quite satisfied the inner man, but Wilde won easily on points. He had a double of everything, and finished up with two cups of tea!

To me, the most interesting feature of that day was the manner in which Wilde passed the hours. We reached Paddington at one o'clock, and made straight for our hotel, where Wilde again showed signs of hunger. Having had another snack, Wilde actually grew boastful, declaring he could always beat me at billiards- and I may as well confess he is a better player than I am, his best break being close on a hundred. Before starting the game, Wilde's manager warned me to see he was not late in reaching Hoxton Baths, but it was close on three o'clock when we left the saloon.

Any other boxer would have taken a rest before a big contest; but Wilde is not "any other boxer." He is just an oddity, a freak; and though I have tried to study him as closely as I possibly can, he is just as much a puzzle today as he was seven or eight years ago.

I have warned him on many occasions not to take risks, and he simply changed the subject. It was three o'clock when we finished our billiards, and he suddenly conceived the idea of having a shave. I waited in the Strand for what I thought was a reasonable time, and at last I went in search of him. Jimmy was calmly having a haircut and shampoo!

By this time I was in a state of great anxiety; but Wilde was quite cool, and when I hailed a taxi and asked the driver to "Let her go!" Jimmy remarked: "There's plenty of time!" It was now nearly four o'clock, and when we reached our destination a great crowd thronged the doors in the hope of seeing Wilde.

Entering the building, we found seats at the ring-side, and twice I had to remind Wilde that it was time he went to the dressing-room. I will not dwell upon the contest, which ended in Wilde knocking Smith out in the third round, but one thing tickled me immensely. As the gloves were being put on, Wilde actually yawned! I had read of giants doing that kind of thing when awakened from a sound sleep, but this boxing microbe is not a giant-he is a giant-killer.

Anyhow, Wilde has Smith at his mercy, and if I required evidence of it, I had it during the brief period of the contest. Smith appeared ready to take a chance in the second round by mixing it, and at once the crowd became tremendously excited. But what of Wilde? He merely ducked a vicious left, allowed Smith to push him, looked over his shoulder at me-and winked! Can you imagine such a situation?

I have never met a boxer who could size up a situation quicker or better than the Tylorstown Terror. I was refereeing a Jimmy Wilde match at Aberdare on one occasion, and his opponent was a sturdy naval stoker, whose massive, tattooed limbs betokened great strength. Wilde kept shooting lefts at this plucky fellow, and was rapidly bringing him down to weight, which means reducing the handicap in avoirdupois by weakening your man, when the stoker suddenly pointed out to me that Wilde's glove was undone. In my experience it is a rare thing for a boxer to call attention to a lace; but Wilde showed me he knew the reason, for, as I hastily stepped up to the Welsh wizard and retied the glove, Wilde coolly remarked: "I expect he wants a spell!"

As a matter of fact, the sailor, soon after resuming, threw out distress signals, and I did not allow the contest to go very far. I hope I shall not be accused of partiality, but I have always maintained that the hardest battles ever fought by Wilde were against Welsh lads.

In the light of his great tussle with Young Symonds, and his defeat at the hands of Tancy Lee, this is a big and bold thing to say; but, first of all, you must remember that the majority of Wilde's contests were fought in a twelve-foot ring. Under such a handicap, he had no room for footwork, with which to avoid punishment, and when he first justified the title of the "Terror," opponents of all sorts and sizes were brought up against him. Weight was seldom taken into account, and I well remember a very good boxer named Hardwick-who scaled over nine stone, and also came from Tylorstown, which in itself is a recommendation-being matched to stand up for eight rounds with Wilde. It was the most remarkable of all Wilde's contests. Time after time he appeared to have

Hardwick at his mercy, but suddenly Wilde himself would be in danger, and, amidst a scene which really baffles description, Hardwick lasted until the final bell, and tottered to his seat. He had lasted the distance, but only at a price.

Charles Barnett

Expert Opinions on Jimmy Wilde

'The greatest fighter of all time must be Jimmy Wilde, with Sugar Ray Robinson being a close second. They both had all the boxing skills, fast hands and feet, good head movement and defence and a real knockout punch in either hand. What gives Wilde the edge is that he gave such large amounts of weight away, beating top class bantam and featherweights, often by stoppage. Pedlar Palmer, known as the 'Box of Tricks' said that Wilde could do things that he 'didn't know were possible'. Wilde was also good enough to box with his hands by his sides, making his man miss – but would put up his guard to "show respect to his opponent" as he himself put it.'

Harold Alderman M.B.E.

'It is a thousand pities that Jimmy Wilde is not a little bigger, and that he has few hopes of ever being substantially bigger. If he could only scale nine stone at the rate he is boxing now, he might *reasonably be expected to win the Heavy-weight Championship of the World.'*

J.G.H Lynch

'Jimmy Wilde, being a Welshman, you would naturally expect to have a lot to say about things, and especially boxing. In the ring Wilde was a revolutionist, the apostle of unorthodoxy and destruction, but outside of it he was rather mum as a rule. He preferred to express himself like most geniuses do, by his work rather than by his tongue.'

Fred Dartnell

'Much has been said and written of Jimmy Wilde's achievements in the boxing-ring, but I unhesitatingly say that nothing more than justice has been done to his fine spirit of fairness, his chivalry to opponents and his magnificent courage.'

Ted Lewis (Manager)

'Jimmy Wilde. I write the name of the greatest flyweight the world has known without caring much whether my selection is universally agreed with or not, for I am convinced in my own mind that he stood absolutely and completely alone.'

Trevor Wignall

'Of this wonderful, strange, uncanny Welshman, it is impossible to employ words to express our admiration; we can only say that his name will endure for all time.'

A.F. Bettinson & B. Bennison

'Jimmy Wilde was a law unto himself, and flouted everything set down in text-books. I have heard that he once knocked out an opponent while his own two feet were off the ground. I am almost prepared to believe it, for he was even a greater freak than Albert Griffiths, known as 'Griffo'.

Charlie Rose

'He was never approached, let alone mastered, on equal terms. As a stylist he was indescribable. He could box like a Driscoll or stand toe to toe and trade punches like one of the primitive pit-fighters from whose ranks he had won his way to the pinnacles, but his special genius lay in fighting in retreat, a shadowy, spindly starveling, noiselessly sliding out of range of great bombardments to pin-point his counter-attack with exquisite shrewdness and finality.'

Denzil Batchelor

'His boxing was unlike any other boxing ever seen anywhere, for undoubtedly he had a sixth

sense which enabled him to anticipate his opponents' moves. His defence was unassailable, and he could hit almost like a heavy-weight. He was always fighting out of his weight, but it seemed to make little difference. His opponents all ended upon the floor.'

Viscount Knebworth

'If ever the term "genius" could be applied to a boxer, then Jimmy Wilde is the boxer who best deserves it.'

Eugene Corri

'Because of his terrific punching powers and unorthodox methods, Wilde has often been described as a fighting freak. But he was not. A pugilistic marvel - yes. A glovefighting genius - yes. But a freak - definitely no. Jimmy Wilde was more, much more, than that. There will never be another Jimmy Wilde. He was the greatest gamecock boxing will ever know.'

James Butler

'Without any doubt, Jimmy Wilde was the greatest flyweight of the age. There was never anything like him before and there has certainly been nothing like him since. Yes, the famous Welshman stood in a class by himself. He made a name for those who battle around 8 st., at the same time building up a reputation that will

never be forgotten. Jimmy Wilde was incomparable, and it is to be doubted if there will ever be another to equal him in fame and popularity.'

Gilbert E. Odd

'In proportion to weight I can recall no greater fighting force than Wilde was at his best. I believe that, if we are to find a boxer who definitely stands out above his predecessors, it is to Wilde more than anyone else that we have to turn. For a 7st. 4lb. man to concede a stone is equivalent to a big man conceding some 3st; yet this is what Wilde was always doing, and that to the best men in the world.'

Norman Clark

'Wherever men fight, and wherever men talk of boxing, the pallid little Welsh collier, Jimmy Wilde, is established as a legend-beyond the mists of memory, beyond the rust of time.'

Reg Gutteridge

JIMMY WILDE

World Flyweight Champion 1916 - 1923
Born : 15th May 1892   Died : 10th March 1969

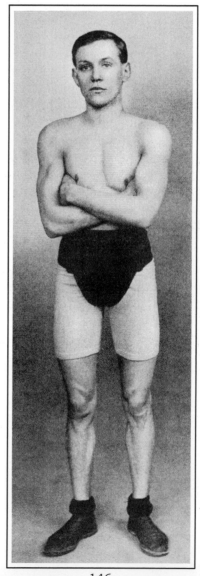

Jimmy Wilde's Statistics

TALE OF THE TAPE

Age:	28 years
Weight:	106 lbs
Height:	5ft 2 ½ inches
Reach:	68 inches
Chest (Normal):	32 ½ inches
Chest (Expanded):	34 ½ inches
Neck:	12 ¾ inches
Thigh:	15 ½ inches
Waist:	22 inches
Calf:	10 ¼ inches
Ankle:	8 ¼ inches
Biceps:	10 ¾ inches
Forearm:	10 ¾ inches
Wrist:	6 ½ inches

*(Taken Before Frank Mason Fight,
March 12th 1920, Toledo, OH, USA)*

JIMMY WILDE

Boxing Record

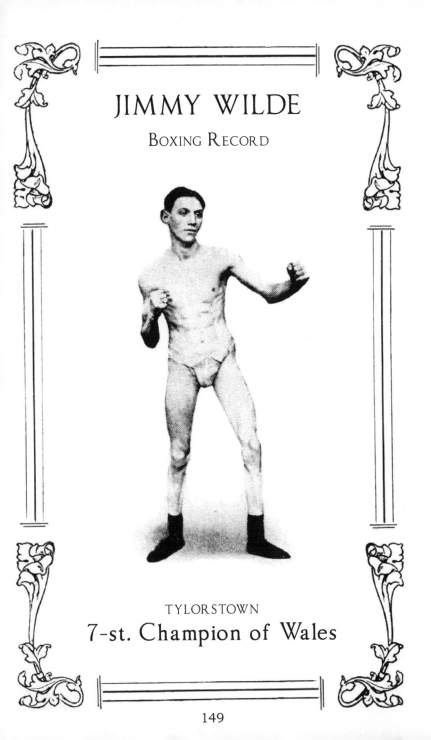

TYLORSTOWN

7-st. Champion of Wales

JIMMY WILDE
Professional Fight Record

1910

Dec 26	Les Williams	Pontypridd Wales	NC ND 3

1911

Jan 1	Ted Roberts	Pontypridd Wales	W KO 3
Jan 10	Dick Jenkins	Pontypridd Wales	W PTS 6
Jan 20	Dai Jones	Pontypridd Wales	D PTS 6
Feb 2	Kid Pearson	Pontypridd Wales	W KO 2
Feb 18	George Lake	Pontypridd Wales	D PTS 6
Mar 9	Dick Jenkins	Cardiff Wales	W PTS 6
Mar 30	Dai Thomas	Pontypridd Wales	W KO 3
Apr 4	Archie Grant	Pontypridd Wales	W KO 3
Apr 10	Eddie Thomas	Pontypridd Wales	W KO 2
Apr 20	Billy Papke	Pontypridd Wales	W KO 3
May 5	Dai Roberts	Pontypridd Wales	W KO 3
May 15	Archie Grant	Pontypridd Wales	W KO 3
May 25	Ted Roberts	Pontypridd Wales	W KO 2
Jun 3	Billy Brown	Pontypridd Wales	W KO 4
Jun 20	Kid Morris	Pontypridd Wales	W PTS 6
Jul 7	Steve Thomas	Pontypridd Wales	W KO 3

Handwritten annotations: "+ 23.2.1911" (near Feb 18/Mar 9), "X" marks (near Mar 30), "W BOWEN" (below May 5)

KEY		
W = Won	DQ = Disqualified	W PTS = Won On Points
L = Lost	KO = Knock Out	TKO = Technical Knock Out
D = Drawn	RTD = Retired	NWS = Newspaper Decision

Aug 8	Fred Chappell	Pontypridd Wales	W PTS 6
Aug 15	James Easton	Edinburgh Scotland	W PTS 10
Aug 26	Dick Jenkins	Pontypridd Wales	W KO 11
Sep 9	Frank Avent	Pontypridd Wales	W KO 4
Sep 20	Ted Powell	Pontypridd Wales	W KO 3
Oct 10	Joe Rogers	Pontypridd Wales	W KO 5
Oct 20	Young Powell	Pontypridd Wales	W KO 3
Oct 30	Young Langford	Pontypridd Wales	W KO 2
Nov 11	Young Towell	Pontypridd Wales	W KO 4
Nov 20	Young Rice	Pontypridd Wales	W KO 4
Dec 12	Young Towell	Pontypridd Wales	W KO 3
Dec 20	Ted Roberts	Pontypridd Wales	W KO 4
Dec 30	Young Jennings	Pontypridd Wales	W PTS 12

1912

Jan 20	Matt Wells' 'Nipper'	The Ring London, England	W KO 1
Feb 1	Young Baker	Liverpool Stadium England	W PTS 6
Feb 15	Young Jennings	Pontypridd Wales	W PTS 6
Mar 9	Young Jennings	Cardiff Wales	W PTS 6
Apr 4	Rowland Hall	U.K.	W KO 4
Jun 3	Joe Wilson	N. Sporting Club London, England	NC ND 6
Jun 20	Lewis Williams	Pavilion Tonypandy, Wales	W KO 5
Jul 20	Kid Morris	National A.C. Cardiff, Wales	W RTD 4
Aug 10	Joe Gans Jr.	Pavilion Tonypandy, Wales	W KO 5

Date	Opponent	Venue	Result
Aug 17	Jim Stuckey	Pavilion Tonypandy, Wales	W KO 8
Sep 19	Walter Hall	Sheffield England	W KO 3
Nov 4	Mike Flynn	Pavilion Tonypandy, Wales	W KO 8
Nov 9	Phil Davies	Drill Hall Merthyr, Wales	W KO 2
Nov 13	Llewellyn Boswell	Swansea Wales	W PTS 6
Nov 16	Young Rainsford	Pavilion Tonypandy, Wales	W KO 2
Nov 30	Alf Williams	Pentre Wales	W PTS 12
Dec 14	Stoker Staines	Pavilion Tonypandy, Wales	W KO 1
Dec 21	Billy Yates	Cardiff Wales	W KO 5
Dec 29	Harry Stuckey	Pavilion Tonypandy, Wales	W KO 1
Dec 31	Billy Padden	National AC Glasgow, Scotland	W KO 18

1913

Date	Opponent	Venue	Result
Jan 18	Tommy Hughes	Hippodrome Tonypandy, Wales	W KO 7
Feb 1	Dick Jenkins	Pavilion Tonypandy, Wales	NC ND 10
Feb 8	Young Tony	Pavilion Tonypandy, Wales	NC ND 10
Feb 15	Kid Fitzpatrick	Pavilion Tonypandy, Wales	W KO 2
Feb 22	Ben Hardwick	Pavilion Tonypandy, Wales	NC ND 8
Mar 1	Harry Stuckey	Pavilion Tonypandy, Wales	NC ND 6
Mar 8	Dai Matthews	Pavilion Tonypandy, Wales	W KO 4
Mar 13	Billy Rowlands	Pentre Wales	NC ND 6
Mar 31	Harry Taylor	Swansea Wales	W KO 3
Apr 12	Will Rees	Pavilion Tonypandy, Wales	W KO 2
May 19	Billy Yates	Pavilion Tonypandy, Wales	W KO 3

May 24	Dai Davies	Pavilion Tonypandy, Wales	W PTS 12
Jun 14	Billy Padden	Pavilion Tonypandy, Wales	W PTS 15
Jun 21	Gwilym Thomas	Pavilion Tonypandy, Wales	W KO 5
Jul 1	Dick Lewis	Pavilion Tonypandy, Wales	W KO 3
Jul 12	Tommy Lewis	Pavilion Tonypandy, Wales	W PTS 12
Jul 19	'Young' Dando (George)	Pavilion Tonypandy, Wales	W PTS 12
Aug 4	Darkey Saunders	Westgate Rink Cardiff, Wales	W PTS 15
Aug 13	Harry Brooks	Manchester England	W KO 8
Aug 28	Young Dyer	Liverpool Stadium England	W KO 3
Sep 6	Dick Jenkins	Ferndale Wales	W PTS 10
Sep 8	Dido Gains	Westgate Rink Cardiff, Wales	W PTS 10
Sep 11	Harry Curley	Victoria Hall Hanley, England	W KO 12
Sep 18	Kid Levine	Victoria Hall Hanley, England	W KO 17
Sep 22	'Young' Dando (George)	Westgate Rink Cardiff, Wales	W PTS 20
Nov 1	Darkey Saunders	Pavilion Tonypandy, Wales	W KO 11
Nov 13	Young Baker	Liverpool Stadium England	W TKO 10
Nov 21	Young Dyer	Manchester England	W KO 2
Nov 22	Dido Gains	Drill Hall Swansea, Wales	W PTS 15
Dec 6	'Young' Dando (George)	Drill Hall Swansea, Wales	W DQ 10
Dec 13	Billy Charles	Pavilion Tonypandy, Wales	W KO 6
Dec 16	Harry Brooks	Free Trade Hall Manchester, England	W RTD 9
Dec 24	Kid Levine	Pavilion Tonypandy, Wales	W KO 8

1914

Jan 3	Kid Nutter	Pavilion Tonypandy, Wales	W PTS 20
Jan 8	Young Beynon	Liverpool Stadium England	W PTS 15
Jan 29	Billy Padden	Liverpool Stadium England	W TKO 3
Feb 2	Kid Nutter	Drill Hall Birkenhead, England	W PTS 15
Feb 9	Tom Thomas	Free Trade Hall Manchester, England	W TKO 7
Feb 12	Paddy Carroll	Liverpool Stadium England	W KO 2
Feb 16	George Jaggers	Sheffield England	W KO 5
Mar 26	Bill Kyne	Liverpool Stadium England	W KO 4
Mar 30	Eugene Husson	N. Sporting Club London, England	W KO 6
Apr 13	Jack Madden	Ashton under Lyne AC England	W KO 4
Apr 16	Albert Bouzonnie	Liverpool Stadium England	W KO 6
Apr 27	Alf Mansfield	Leeds England	W PTS 20
May 11	Georges Gloria	N. Sporting Club London, England	W TKO 9
Jun 22	Charlie Banyard	Market Hall Aberdare, Wales	W KO 9
Jul 18	Charley Jordan	Pavilion Tonypandy, Wales	W KO 10
Jul 23	Artie Edwards	Liverpool Stadium England	W PTS 15
Aug 19	Young Baker	Granby Halls Leicester, England	W PTS 15
Sep 28	Alf Mansfield	N. Sporting Club London, England	W KO 10
Nov 16	Joe Symonds	N. Sporting Club London, England	W PTS 15
Dec 3	Sid Smith	Liverpool Stadium England	W KO 9

1915

Jan 25	Tancy Lee	N. Sporting Club London, England	L TKO 17
Mar 25	Sid Shields	Liverpool Stadium England	W KO 2
Jul 24	Driver Benthew	Sheffield England	W KO 5
Aug 14	George Clarke	Sheffield England	W KO 8
Sep 23	Walter Buchanan	Liverpool Stadium England	W KO 5
Oct 20	Peter Cullen	Dublin Ireland	W KO 9
Nov 27	Tommy Hughes	Barrow In Furness England	W RTD 8
Dec 9	Johnny Best	Liverpool Stadium England	W TKO 14
Dec 16	Danny Elliot	Bradford England	W KO 2
Dec 20	Sid Smith	N. Sporting Club London, England	W TKO 8

1916

Jan 8	Billy Rowlands	Swansea Wales	W KO 7
Jan 24	Tommy Noble	New Cross Baths London, England	W KO 11
Jan 27	Jimmy Morton	Liverpool Stadium England	W KO 2
Feb 14	Joe Symonds	N. Sporting Club London, England	W RTD 12
Mar 9	Sam Kellar	W. London Stadium London, England	W KO 8
Mar 27	Sid Smith	Hoxton Baths London, England	W KO 3
Apr 24	Johnny Rosner	Liverpool Stadium England	W RTD 11
Apr 29	Benny Thomas	Cardiff Wales	W PTS 20
May 13	Joe Magnus	Woolwich Labour Club London, England	W KO 2
May 13	Darkey Saunders	Woolwich Labour Club London, England	W TKO 3
May 29	Tommy Harrison	Oxford Music Hall London, England	W KO 8

Jun 26	Tancy Lee	N. Sporting Club London, England	W TKO 11
Jul 31	Johnny Hughes	Kensal Rise Grounds London, England	W KO 15
Nov 9	Tommy Noble	Liverpool Stadium England	W KO 15
Dec 18	Young Zulu Kid	Holborn Stadium London, England	W TKO 11

1917

Mar 11	George Clark	N. Sporting Club London, England	W TKO 4
Mar 22	Frankie Russell	Holborn Stadium London, England	W KO 3

1918

Mar 28	Corporal Jacobs	Theatre Royal Aldershot, England	W KO 4
Apr 29	Dick Heasman	N. Sporting Club London, England	W RTD 2
Aug 31	Joe Conn	Stamford Bridge London, England	W TKO 12
Dec 11	Digger Evans	Royal Albert Hall London, England	W PTS 3
Dec 11	Joe Lynch	Royal Albert Hall London, England	W PTS 3
Dec 12	Pal Moore	Royal Albert Hall London, England	L PTS 3

1919

Mar 31	Joe Lynch	N. Sporting Club London, England	W PTS 15
Apr 21	Jimmy Buck	Liverpool Stadium England	W KO 3
May 16	Alf Mansfield	Holborn Stadium London, England	W RTD 13
Jul 17	Pal Moore	Olympia, London England	W PTS 20
Dec 6	Jack Sharkey	Auditorium Milwaukee, WI, U.S.	L NWS 10

1920

Jan 8	Babe Asher	Future City A.C. Saint Louis, MO, U.S.	W NWS 8
Jan 29	Mike Ertle	Auditorium Milwaukee, WI, U.S.	W KO 3

Feb 19	Mickey Russell	4th Regiment Armory Jersey City, NJ, U.S.	W TKO 7
Mar 3	Patsy Wallace	National A.C. Philadelphia, PA, U.S.	W NWS 6
Mar 12	Frankie Mason	Coliseum, Toledo, OH, U.S	W NWS 12
Apr 12	Young Zulu Kid	Windsor Ontario, Canada	W NWS 10
Apr 21	Battling Murray	Sportsman's Club Camden, NJ, U.S.	W TKO 8
May 1	Bobby Dyson	Cuddy's Arena Lawrence, MA, U.S.	W KO 1
May 13	Battling Murray	National A.C. Philadelphia, PA, U.S.	W KO 2
May 24	Patsy Wallace	Toronto Ontario, Canada	W PTS 10

1921

| Jan 13 | Pete Herman | Royal Albert Hall London, England | L TKO 17 |

1923

| Jun 18 | Pancho Villa | Polo Grounds New York, NY, U.S. | L KO 7 |

KEY		
W = Won	DQ = Disqualified	W PTS = Won On Points
L = Lost	KO = Knock Out	TKO = Technical Knock Out
D = Drawn	RTD = Retired	NWS = Newspaper Decision

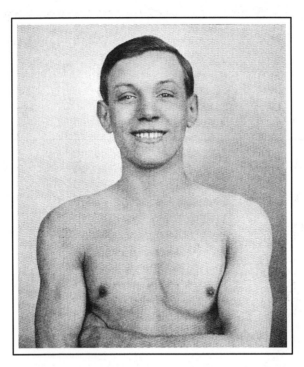

GENI(US) OF THE RING

The Maxim of Jimmy Wilde

Sports writer Trevor Wignall once asked Jimmy Wilde
for a statement that he could repeat to a group of schoolboys
to whom he was going to give an inspirational talk,
Wilde replied:

"Live a clean life, give everyone a square deal,
fight as hard as you can, and then,
if you do not win all your contests,
you will at least keep your friends."

Jimmy Wilde